EDGAR CAYCE
ON THE REINCARNATION OF
FAMOUS PEOPLE

A.R.E. MEMBERSHIP SERIES

EDGAR CAYCE ON THE REINCARNATION OF FAMOUS PEOPLE

by Kevin J. Todeschi

ASSOCIATION FOR
RESEARCH AND
ENLIGHTENMENT

A.R.E. Press • Virginia Beach • Virginia

A.R.E. Press
Sixty-Eighth & Atlantic Avenue
P.O. Box 656
Virginia Beach, VA 23451-0656

Todeschi, Kevin J.
   Edgar Cayce on the reincarnation of famous people / by
Kevin J. Todeschi.
       p.   cm.
   Includes bibliographical references.
   ISBN 0-87604-410-0 (pbk.)
   1. Reincarnation—Biography. 2. Cayce, Edgar, 1877-1945.
I. Title.
BL519. T63   1998
133.9'01'35—dc21   98-17669

The A.R.E. Membership Series

This book, *Edgar Cayce on the Reincarnation of Famous People,* is another in a continuing series of books that is published by the Association for Research and Enlightenment, Inc., for individuals who are especially interested in their personal and spiritual growth and transformation.

The A.R.E. was founded in 1931 as a nonprofit organization to study, research, and disseminate information on holistic health, vocational guidance, spiritual growth, dreams, meditation, life after death, and dozens of other subjects. The A.R.E. continues its mission today, nurturing a worldwide membership with conferences, study groups, and a variety of publications—all aimed at helping seekers find paths that will lead to a more fulfilling life, mentally, physically, and spiritually. The hallmark of A.R.E.'s publications is to be helpful and hopeful.

Many of the books published by A.R.E. are available in bookstores throughout the world and all are available directly from the A.R.E.'s mail-order catalogs.

Three new books in this *A.R.E. Membership Series* are sent as gifts each year to individuals who are Sponsoring members or Life members of A.R.E. Each of the titles in this series will become available, in the year after initial publication, for purchase by individuals throughout the world who are interested in individual growth and transformation.

For more information about membership benefits of the nonprofit Association for Research and Enlightenment, Inc., please turn to the last page in this volume.

The A.R.E. Membership Series:

Contents

Introduction

Of the more than 14,000 readings given by Edgar Cayce over a forty-three-year period, approximately 2,000 deal with the subject of reincarnation. From Cayce's perspective, each of us goes through a series of lifetimes for the express purpose of soul growth and development. In that process, the soul is given opportunities and experiences which will best enable the individual to fulfill the purpose for which he or she incarnated. In the language of the readings, the individual is given whatever conditions are needed, "to meet the needs of that to make the entity at an at oneness with the Creative Energy." (254-32)

The readings on reincarnation were given to individuals in order to help them understand soul strengths and weaknesses, as well as their own potentials and challenges. As Cayce entered his trance state, he was given a specific suggestion that enabled him to access the necessary information for a "life reading," which dealt with the soul's history. That suggestion was as follows:

"You will have before you the life existence in the earth plane (giving name, date, where) and the earthly existence of this entity in that of (giving name and place of the earthly sojourn) and you will give a biographical life of the entity in that day and plane of earthly existence, from entrance and how into the earth's plane and the entity's departure, giving the development or retarding points in such an existence." 254-22

Cayce's response to that suggestion would provide the individual with a historical timeline of her or his incarnations, lessons learned, as well as any faults or patterns that had been acquired and needed to be overcome in the present.

Critics of reincarnation often point out that everyone believes she or he was a Cleopatra, a George Washington, or some famous personage from the annals of history. Whatever happened to all of the common people? Where are all the farmers, the housewives, the peasants, the prisoners, or the uneducated masses that made up the bulk of history's population? Although the Cayce readings did give a number of famous identities from the past, the majority of the life readings are filled with names of individuals who were everyday people. In fact, of the more than 10,000 names given in past-life readings, less than 2 percent are identifiable as "famous" and approximately half of that number are characters from the Bible.

For those individuals who are certain that they were someone famous from the past, it's important to point out a commonly overlooked aspect of the "famous person syndrome." Oftentimes, individuals are drawn to others because they are responding to patterns of human experience and behavior. Very often, a person in the present resonates to someone from the past, not because he or she was that person but because the historical figure represents or corresponds to something in the individual's present lifetime. Another possibility is that a person's present-day connection with a past-life identity is not because the person was that individual, but rather because the present-day person was once familiar with that famous individual. One example from the readings is the case of a forty-seven-year-old man, [1151], who was convinced he was the reincarnation of President James A. Garfield. Another psychic had even confirmed this connection. However, Cayce stated in reading 1151-4 that the individual had simply been a very close associate of Garfield's and not the president himself.

Regardless of an individual's present circumstance, Cayce believed that each lifetime could be a purposeful experience. To be sure, the soul takes with it all memories, talents, and shortcomings acquired in previous experiences, but the present—and how an individual responds to experiences in the here and now—is much more important than anything that went before. The past merely provides a framework of potentials and probabilities. From the readings' perspective, one purpose for delving into the history of an entity was simply as a means of discovering the continuity of the soul.

With the premise that we might somehow glimpse aspects of this continuity by reviewing the soul histories of others, this volume presents an overview of those readings that identified the individual as having some notoriety at some point in history. It does not include case histories for biblical personages or those individuals for whom no contemporary reference or verification is available; nor does it include identities for those individuals who were related to or simply associated with a famous person; only those individuals who were given notable identities themselves have been included.

FAMOUS PEOPLE MENTIONED

Achilles
ca. Twelfth Century B.C.
Case 900

According to Greek mythology, Achilles was the bravest, strongest, and most competent Greek hero of the Trojan War. When he was an infant, every part of his body (except for the heel by which his mother held him) had been dipped into the River Styx, thus making him nearly invulnerable. He killed the great Trojan hero, Hector, and died shortly thereafter when an arrow pierced his heel.

Apparently, Achilles was a real individual as well as a figure from mythology for in 1924, a twenty-nine-year-old stockbroker was told that he had been Achilles. Self-certain, intelligent, and wealthy, he was told in his reading: "One upon whom many will rely for their mental activities in the Earth's forces. One that is given especially to being the control in many financial undertakings." (900-6)

In his life as Achilles, [900] had never met Helen of Troy, although he constantly held her up as an ideal since she was the reason for which the Greeks and Trojans were fighting. In his present life, [900] found himself married to [136], who had been Helen of Troy. Although he idealized his wife and considered himself her protector, because he had once been killed fighting for Helen's honor, subconsciously he sometimes felt that the beauty and power of such a woman could be dangerous. The two later divorced. (See also "Helen of Troy.")

Six months after his first life reading, [900] obtained a follow-up reading on his Grecian incarnation as Achilles:

> In the entrance into the earth's plane in that of, or called, Achilles, we find in the period of earthly existences when conditions were accentuated along certain lines. The entity then as the male offspring and entered in with the beauties of the rustic nature of the time and place, near Athenia or Athens, and raised to manhood, or young manhood, in and about the Mount, and given all advantages in the exercises and games and learning of the day, with the beauties of that in that day as could be obtained by one that was raised for the special purpose of entering into the political, social and other conditions of day and age. Soon learned that of the soldier with the spear, bow and axe, with an armor as prepared by the mother of the body, and given all the benefits of the aristocrats of the age, given exceptional abilities and applied same in the moral, physical, development of the body. One, then, beautiful of stature, physical, mind and of the expressing of same. Soon drawn in early manhood into the political situations surrounding the conditions of the country, coming then as a companion to many of the leaders in that day when there were personal combats in every phase of the physical prowess of the body. The entity showing the exceptional abilities of the environments under which the body had been developed in the day when this, the development of physical prowess, was studied and given the greater extent of attention. In personal combats often the body [was] successful and called the leader of the army and group, or the per-

sonal representative of the armies of the entity in the reign of those in charge of same at time.

In the social and moral life, we find the entity one showing development in mental abilities. One showing development in moral conditions, as is shown in the relation to captives as were taken by the armies and distributed, the favorites to the favorite of the army. In the personal combats we find the exceptional abilities in mental forces also shown. The entity then departed the life in personal combat, wounded in the heel, from which gangrene set in in body and became blood poison to the system. In the day we find much written concerning this entity, and there are given many abilities that are only written in the form of the day and age, as is written of many who show their abilities in a manner that is developing in earth plane toward the spiritual forces to which all strive.

Departing then with only the forces as of not able to meet the needs of physical suffering under the conditions which came to same. Only erring then in that manner. Hence in the present plane the necessity of being able to meet those conditions that would seem to overwhelm the entity, the necessity of, as has been given, "Be still—and listen to the voice from within."   900-63

In this life, [900] was extremely intelligent. He was among the few individuals of Cayce's contemporaries who could easily understand some of the most complicated concepts explored in the readings. He was told that in the past, as Achilles, he had mastered the earth. He had also gained great mental abilities. The challenge for [900] in this life was to apply the achievements he had accomplished over the physical/mental realms and bring a new understanding of oneness and spirituality to the world. For a time, he headed up the work of Cayce's Association, becoming its chief financial backer and the builder of the Cayce Hospital. Extremely interested in higher education, he also founded Atlantic University. Unfortunately, due to personality conflicts and jealousy, [900] would later withdraw from the Association. In time, he would also lose his fortune.

Mr. [900] died in 1954 of a heart attack.

Adams, John Quincy
1767-1848
Case 2167

John Quincy Adams was the son of John Adams, second U.S. president, and would become the sixth president of the United States in 1824. At the time, he was considered the primary architect of U.S. foreign policy. After his presidency, he held a seat in the U.S. House of Representatives from 1831-1848, where he fought consistently against the expansion of slavery.

In 1940, a twenty-three-year-old college student, who was studying diplomacy at George Washington University, was told that he had been John Quincy Adams. After receiving his reading, his mother stated, "Everything regarding his nature, characteristics, etc., is *so* true!" The reading said, in part:

> For as opportunity presents itself to this entity for a service of a nature that requires the analyzing of all phases of man's experience among his fellow men, let it all be tempered with justice, mercy, peace and truth. These are the purposes upon which this land were founded; and they are those forces, those self-evident facts of man's existence that are a part and parcel of every soul's expression in the material plane; that freedom of speech, free-

dom of the purpose for worshipfulness of Creative forces according to the dictates of one's own conscience, shall never perish from the earth . . .

Then, we find one destined—by that *already* accomplished, and the intent and purpose—to be a power, a voice among his fellow men; in strange places, in strange lands—perchance.

Yet, let it be with that purpose for which the entity once took that oath; to sustain those principles, those activities which caused the foundation of this land.

Hence in service for his fellow man, in the raising of the voice for considerations in all walks and all phases of man's experience, we find the channels through which the entity may have an outlet for not only the expansion of his virtues as indicated, but also make for a growth in the knowledge and in the power and the might of one doing God's service among his fellow men . . .

Before this, then, the entity was in the name Adams; John Q., or Quincy. 2167-1

In Rome he had been an interpreter of the law and an advocate of freedom of speech and freedom of activity for all the people. From the Holy Land, [2167] had acquired the innate tendency to be "soulful" about matters in life and as a result he was easily discouraged. In lifetimes in Israel and in Egypt, he had developed an intense interest in spirituality. He was told that his greatest strengths in the present would be as a political economist or a diplomat.

Three years later, in 1943, [2167]'s mother reported that her son was then the youngest officer on the faculty of a tactical school in New Jersey. He was married and had three daughters. No additional follow-up reports are on file.

Alexander the Great
356-323 B.C.
Case 1208

Alexander (III) the Great was one of the greatest conquerors and military leaders the world has ever known. Schooled by the philosopher, Aristotle, he became king of Macedonia at the age of twenty. By the time he died at the age of thirty-three, he controlled an empire that spread from Greece to India and encompassed both the Egyptian and Persian empires.

Parents of a three-day-old boy were told in 1936 that their child's upbringing and education were of the utmost importance. Cayce predicted that if the child were raised properly, his life would be instrumental in helping to create a new world order that could unify humanity. The parents were told that their son had once been two leaders from the past: Alexander the Great and Thomas Jefferson. Although his soul had gained in its incarnation as Jefferson, he had lost as Alexander. (See also "Jefferson, Thomas.")

Before that we find the entity was in that land during those periods when there were the activities that made for the rise and fall of many lands, in the Grecian, the Persian, all of the eastern lands; when *that* entity now known as Alexander the Great made for the conquering forces of the earth—the depleting that there might bring to self the exaltations.

Here the entity lost. For these will become in the experience of the entity those influences that might makes for right, or power making for indulgences. And if these are not conquered in the experiences as the principles that are set in its earthly experience, these may run as wild in the very activities of the entity—even as then.   1208-1

As if foreseeing coming events, the reading warned the parents that their child's opportunities for fame or "those of defame, will be *as one.*" At least seven times in the reading, Cayce reminded the parents of their important role in guiding and directing this child. Unfortunately, [1208]'s parents had an extremely difficult relationship so that the boy never received the stable upbringing he required. Until he was fifteen, he was shuttled among relatives' homes in different states (and various schools) so frequently that he was rarely in the same place for even a year. His difficult childhood made it impossible for him to obtain the potential promised in his reading. Confirming Edgar Cayce's statement that he would "belong . . . to the *world*," his life took him to such places as Japan, Greece, Italy, Spain, and Africa. Although he was personable and people liked him, much of his life seemed spent in trying to find himself.

Audubon, John James
1785-1851
Case 410

John James Audubon was an ornithologist, a naturalist, and an artist who became known for his drawings and paintings of North American birds. His classic work, *The Birds of America*, contains more than 400 handcolored plates. The National Audubon Society, founded in 1905, was named after him.

In April of 1934, a forty-two-year-old widow was told that she had an innate talent for seeing "the beauties that are seen in nature . . . The song of the bird, the beauty of the rose, the buzz of the bee, the activities of those things that give forth in themselves the expressions of the joy of just using—for the time being—a portion of God in their activity." Apparently, she had once been Audubon:

Before this we find the entity was among those peoples that came into this land, where there might be a refuge from the trials first of that they had experienced in the rough voyage on the sea, and in what is now known as Louisiana.

The entity then was among those peoples that found a haven there, and brought to those lands in the latter experience the joys of many, and builded for much that has given joy and peace to the minds and hearts of many who have loved God's little folk in the bird kingdom.

Then, in the name Audubon, the entity made for a home; and when turmoils and strifes came, even through those trials of those that made war—and the changes in the associations, the entity brought to many the faith and hope still in those same powers and influences that had preserved them from the water and from the billow and from the storm; that though the forces in nature may roll and rage they may destroy only the body, and the soul may live on in that which has been the desire.   410-2

Mrs. [410] was told that she possessed broadness of vision and could deeply appreciate anything that grew, anything that was alive or anything that was beautiful to behold, whether it was "the blessings of the afternoon rain or the morning sun." Her talents as an artist and her love for nature had developed in Chaldea when she had learned to appreciate the beauties of everyday life. In ancient Egypt, she had learned of purity and had worked in one of the temples.

In the present, [410] possessed talents as an artist and was encouraged to direct her skill into such things as the creation of booklets or greeting cards and pictures which could bring beauty into the lives of those who were sick, depressed, or in need. She also maintained an interest in a flower business.

Augustus
63 B.C.-A.D. 14
Case 1266

Originally named Gaius Octavius (also known as Octavian), he was the nephew of Julius Caesar. When Octavian was only eighteen, Caesar was assassinated, but in Caesar's will Octavian was named adopted son and heir by his uncle and given the name Gaius Julius Caesar. In the power struggle that followed Caesar's death, he became one of three individuals charged with reorganizing the republic. Shortly thereafter, he and Mark Antony defeated Caesar's assassins and divided the empire amongst themselves. An affair with Cleopatra led to Antony's downfall; and after Gaius Julius Caesar had conquered Egypt (leading to the suicide of both Antony and Cleopatra), he became sole ruler of the Roman Empire. He was given the name Augustus (the Exalted) by the Senate and became known as the first Roman emperor.

Augustus added new territories to the empire and, after years of fighting, managed to bring peace to the country (the Pax Romana). Considered one of the great administrative geniuses of history, he overhauled every aspect of Roman life, bringing prosperity and stability to the empire. During his rule, Augustus revived religious customs and restored a stern sense of morality to the country. As emperor, he sponsored the leading artists and writers of his time and led his empire during what has been called a golden age. After death, he became deified.

In 1936, the son-in-law of a seventy-six-year-old manufacturer convinced his father-in-law to obtain a life reading. Experiencing financial and business challenges, Mr. [1266] was the head of a large rubber company in the middle of a restructuring and takeover. Cayce began the reading by stating that [1266] had made some progress in overcoming a soul tendency to place himself above others. In a life just previous to the present, he had been named Samuel Goldenson and was very active in the cause which brought the colonies together in order to overcome British rule. In fact, Cayce stated that it was Goldenson who first uttered the statement, "taxation without representation *is* tyranny." In a life in France, he had also fought against taxation by the ruling class at the expense of the common people.

Apparently these two lives had helped to balance a tremendous ego and the sense that [1266] was somehow better than others. Cayce stated that this individual had been the Roman emperor Augustus:

> Before that the entity was as Caesar Augustus, who made for the great expansions of the Roman land not only for power but for the gratifying of the ego of self; and those periods when the great expansions of that land arose.
>
> The entity then was that one who builded for that empire.
>
> And there is felt innately in every move that those peoples of that land, that are of the *Roman* and not the Italian mixture, are superior in some manner or way. This is *innate*, and yet there is known and must be known within self that the spiritual purposes, the spiritual desires *must* be those that make for the greater forces that manifest in and among men.
>
>   1266-1

In Israel, Mr. [1266] had apparently served as a counselor. His talent with manufacturing and rubber had first developed in Atlantis when he became involved in the production of various products from trees. He was told that even at seventy-six he still had a work to do which was "in helping others to know their true relationships to their Maker or to the Creative Forces, and in the ways and manners of giving expressions of same toward their fellow man." It was a statement which [1266] himself felt drawn to because he later told Mr. Cayce that one of his innate urges was to help people "find their source of power."

Mr. [1266] died in 1955 at the age of ninety-five.

Barrington, George
1755-1844
Case 2213

He was an Irish adventurer who become famous for his abilities as a pickpocket in England. His crimes would eventually see him deported to Australia where he would become superintendent of convicts. By some accounts, he also authored several histories of his adopted Australian home.

In 1926, a woman who had experienced great difficulty raising her unmanageable sixteen-year-old stepson requested a reading. The boy's mother had died, as had the boy's father after his second marriage. Apparently, the boy had run away from home and gone to sea to be an adventurer. A life reading was procured and stated that the child would not return to the United States until he was middle-aged. In the past, the child had developed an innate interest in such things as the sea, mystery, and the love of many lands, firearms, and the occult. She was told that, in the past, her stepson had been the pirate, Captain Kidd. (See also "Kidd, Captain.") One month later while discussing the life readings in general, reading 254-32 suggested that an interesting parallel could be drawn between the lives of George

Barrington and Captain Kidd since they were the same soul.

Boleyn, Anne
ca. 1507-1536
Case 1521

Anne was the second wife of Henry VIII after he divorced Catherine of Aragon and broke with the Roman Catholic Church. At first, Henry was infatuated with Anne, but he lost interest after only a few years of marriage. During their marriage, Anne gave birth to a daughter, Elizabeth, who would eventually become queen, as well as a stillborn son. In 1536, Henry had Anne arrested, tried for adultery, and beheaded.

In 1938, parents of a baby girl were told that their daughter had been Anne Boleyn:

> Before this we find the entity was in the English land, when there were those tenets of the Church and the State that were at a period of disturbance.
> During those experiences the entity then was close in the activities of those that were in authority; being in the name Anne Boleyn, or that one who lost in its attempt to hold *to* those forces and influences that would *hold* to its religion and its moral life, and to that in which it was associated in material and political affairs of the land.   1521-1

In previous lifetimes in the Holy Land, she had developed her intuition and had acquired a personal awareness of the presence of God. She had also served as a prophetess. In ancient Egypt she had been with her father and had assisted him in a rebellion against those in power. Cayce stated that her life direction in the present would be entirely dependent upon the guidance and direction she received as a child.

Although raised in a Catholic home, her father, a writer of some reputation, had a great deal of frustration with many aspects of his religion. [1521]'s parents later obtained physical readings for their daughter on a variety of childhood ailments, including an unusual amount of hair that grew across the back of the child's neck and shoulders. As she grew to adulthood, [1521] maintained an interest in spirituality and would study both Catholicism and Judaism (her husband's religion).

At one point, [1521] became a very successful newspaper reporter. One of the last reports on file states that she and her husband had two sons and that she had just been accepted to law school.

Brutus, Marcus Junius
ca. 85-42 B.C.
Case 1976

Brutus achieved fame for his part in the conspiracy that resulted in the assassination of Julius Caesar. A skilled politician, he was admired by his contemporaries for his idealism. He loved the republic which was Rome, although he was extreme in his financial dealings with others. Philosophically opposed to assassinations, he joined the conspiracy against Caesar nonetheless in the hopes of restoring a republican government. When it became clear that the republic would remain an empire under Antony and Octavian, he committed suicide.

In 1939, just before [1976] was about to be born, the child's father went out to a small stationery store to buy some birth announcements. While he was waiting to make his purchase, his eyes scanned a row of books. Even though he had not read more than one or two books since college, he was suddenly overcome with the desire to buy one of the volumes on the shelf. The book was *The Life of Julius Caesar.* Later, his wife made fun of him because she had never seen him read a book. When it came time for his wife's labor, the man took the book with him to the waiting room of the hospital and read it while his wife gave birth. Imagine the couple's surprise when a life reading for the baby at one month stated that their son had been Brutus:

> One that will need discipline, and even in the early stages the routine as a soldier or those characters of conditions that make for such should be the rule of the life in its formative experience; else the entity may become a wanderer.
>
> For there is the inclination to see and be a part of so many affairs.
>
> Hence we will see more and more that of hero worship, even in the early years of the experience . . .
>
> The name in that period was Brutus—hence the divisions and yet the longings to be as Caesar in that experience.
>
> Then, let the entity learn discipline—teach the entity discipline from every angle—but in love, in patience.   1976-1

Cayce stated that the child would tend to be materialistic and that he would be strong in body and mind and determined to have his own way in life. Throughout the reading Cayce emphasized that the child needed discipline and guidance or else he would have the tendency to become a "wanderer." For that reason, when [1976] was older he was encouraged to receive some routine military training.

Throughout his formative years, the boy was seen as a model child. He did well in school and became president of his high school class as well as a class officer in college. Graduating with honors, he joined the ROTC and spent two years in the navy as a commissioned officer. Eventually he did labor relations work for a public utility company and was successful. Desiring to get ahead faster, he eventually switched careers to life insurance and investment funds, where he did very well.

By all accounts, [1976] was always interested in civic affairs and had a "natural bent and flair for this type of thing." Over the years, he headed up PTAs and funded political campaigns; his father predicted that eventually [1976] would run for political office on a national scale.

No additional reports are on file.

Bulwer-Lytton, Edward George
1803-1873
Case 3657

Edward George Bulwer-Lytton (First Baron Lytton) was a member of the English Parliament and a writer of historical romances, novels, and plays. His works include *The Last Days of Pompeii* (1834) and *Richelieu* (1839).

A fifty-eight-year-old jeweler and optometrist was told that his talent with gems and precious metals could be traced to a life he had lived in Egypt "as a carver of gold, a carver of stones—as of rubies, diamonds, emeralds and those prepared for those in authority and in power." However, over the years he had become dissatisfied with his occupation and longed to do something else, but he didn't know what. His discontent and unhappiness had even led to a bout with alcohol, which he had overcome. His reading stated that he had great talents that had gone untapped:

Here we have an unusual individuality—and he's certainly missed his calling!

While there are those tendencies, inclinations, abilities in any scientific or mechanical activities, the greater abilities of the entity might, in this experience have been expended in a constructive manner, as heretofore, as an author. For this was one Bulwer-Lytton!   3657-1

He had also acquired an interest in things of a mechanical nature from a lifetime in Greece when he served in the military.

Mr. [3657] was told that he could produce even greater works than he had as Bulwer-Lytton, if he would simply put his mind to writing. In response to the suggestion, [3657] later wrote, "I have often felt the urge to write stories but it never was a necessity that I try." According to the files, Mr. [3657] lived to the age of seventy-four and remained active in his business until a few days prior to his death in 1960. There is no record as to whether or not he ever tried his hand at writing.

Years later, in 1976, his daughter wrote and stated that she had just finished a Bulwer-Lytton novel and was amazed because it "was [just] like listening to Daddy talk!"

Burr, Aaron
1756-1836
Case 1235

Aaron Burr was the third vice-president of the United States (under Thomas Jefferson) and is best known for having killed his political rival, Alexander Hamilton, in a duel. Although he served out his four-year vice-presidency well, afterward his political career was marked by foreign intrigue and failed treason against the United States. His own desire for power proved his undoing. He was acquitted of treason, a capital offense, only because his plots had been thwarted before being committed. After his political ambitions were over, he spent some time in Europe before returning to the United States to practice law until his death. (See also "Hamilton, Alexander.")

A thirteen-year-old boy was told that he possessed innate abilities as an orator and a politician that had been developed during lifetimes in Rome and at the founding of the United States:

> For as we find a political career should be that for the greater training, for the greater development, for the greater abilities, for the greater possibilities for the entity in this experience.
>
> For as the activities have guided, do guide the experiences of others, and as the experiences have been in such an environ, those inclinations will be in such ways and manners as *helpful*—if the purposes, the ideals of the entity are held in those directions as to make for the *correcting* of self first, then the aiding in correcting the moral, the economic, the social order for others . . .
>
> Before this, then, we find the entity was *that* one known as Aaron Burr; of which so much is known that little may be added to that—but that those things that brought about those experiences in the affairs of the entity during that sojourn may *not* be repeated. For these will come as experiences, the urges for repeating of those that questioned the entity, even as then.   1235-1

The reading stated that innately [1235] could be quite headstrong. Cayce encouraged the boy's parents to persuade by reason and logic rather than by power or might, for he would rebel against any forcefulness. Although he had often been associated with those in power in the past, Cayce said his activities are "not well-spoken of in many circles." His guardians were advised to guide him in the direction of law and political science. Rather than learning political might and the force of power, he was to be guided in learning how politics could be used for creating peace and harmony. He needed to discover how the state could direct individuals in their service toward one another.

According to the reports, [1235] never did learn law or go to college. Instead, he married early and had several children. He eventually entered the civil service and worked for a naval shipyard. A veteran of World War II, he was buried with full military honors when he died in 1975.

Campbell, Thomas
1763-1854
Case 2547

Thomas Campbell was a Presbyterian minister who immigrated to the United States from Ireland. Eventually, he would become one of the founders and organizers of the Disciples of Christ Church.

In a reading which saw great promise for the child's future, the father of a four year old was told that his son had often been responsible for the manifestation of spiritual truths in the earth. If the child were guided aright, once again he would bring much help and assistance to humankind:

Before this the entity was in the Scotch land. The entity began its activity as a prodigy, as one already versed in its associations with the unseen—or the elemental forces; the fairies and those of every form that do not give expression in a material way and are only seen by those who are attuned to the infinite.

Then the entity in the developing was in the name Thomas Campbell, the reformer in the land of the present nativity; which, as combined later with Barton Stone, brought into activity that known as a denomination.

The intent and purpose was to *unify* all Protestant thought, speaking where the Book spoke, keeping silent where it kept silent upon the activities or associations of individuals in relationships to groups or to masses.   2547-1

Additional lives in the Holy Land had demonstrated that the soul had acquired a deep personal relationship with the Creator, learning how to manifest spiritual principles in the earth. Cayce suggested that [2547] was a great soul and possessed nearly limitless spiritual potential. The boy's parents were encouraged to guide him in matters of spirituality and to acquaint him especially with the stories in the Old and New Testaments.

In 1957, one of the few reports on file states that [2547] had married and that he and his wife were both very active Baptists, each teaching and working in religious education.

Carroll, Charles
1737-1832
Case 3178

An American patriot, Charles Carroll is best known for having been the last surviving signer of the Declaration of Independence and the only Roman Catholic to sign that document. He also served as a U.S. senator from 1789 to 1792.

In 1943, a middle-aged auditor and employee of the U.S. government was interested in obtaining a life reading for himself. Among the questions he submitted was,

"Did I live in America during the American Revolution?" He was told that he had been Charles Carroll: "Before this the entity was in the land of the present nativity when there were turmoils and even the signing of the Declaration of Independence. Then entity was the last to sign . . ."

According to [3178]'s reading, a trend that the individual had often allowed himself to fall into was the habit of waiting "for something to happen," a trait which often led to indecision. In England he had led various groups of people but had often waited to the last minute before making any decision. In Egypt he had taken part in a rebellion and later switched sides to support the very individual against whom he had once rebelled. His affinity for independence was traceable to a life he had lived in Persia when he had been a soldier defending the rights of his home people against invading Greeks. As an aside, Cayce suggested that [3178] learn numerology because—according to the soul's records—the individual had been born on the same day for the last three lifetimes.

He was apparently already in a job well suited for his soul talents which were along the lines of, "Anything that has to do with the handling of campaigns, programs, or things having to do with others' financial status, or as a clerk of a town, community, county, or the like." (3178-1) He was encouraged to work on his tendency toward indecision.

One of the few reports [3178] submitted states: "For some time prior to my 'life reading,' on Aug. 24, 1943, I had been thinking about the similarity between the problems of this Country now and then, I had even thought quite a bit about the place the 'Founding Fathers' have in our present-day life, so you can imagine my feelings when my 'life reading' came."

Cato, Valerius
First Century B.C.
Case 2162

A Roman grammarian and poet, Cato was considered to be the leader of a new school of thought in poetry that emphasized mythological epics and lyrics rather than traditional dramas. In his day, he was thought to be a very talented writer. Although he was frequently complimented for his work by his contemporaries, he died very poor.

An eighteen-year-old boy was told that two of his previous incarnations would be extremely influential in the present: one as the Roman poet, Cato, and the other as the American politician, Cassius Marcellus Clay. (See also "Clay, Cassius Marcellus.") In addition to writing, he was encouraged to study international relations and political science. As to whether or not he could match the reputation he had achieved in the past was dependent upon his application in the present:

> This might apply especially to those experiences when the entity was the politician, Clay; which bring into the present experience of the entity the ability as a speaker, a leader, one with a special interest in political science, or political economics, or those things that would have to do with the activities of peoples in many walks of life, rather than in that as would pertain to mechanics. However, from other experiences in the earth we find that such has been a part of the entity's application, in things pertaining to engineering.
>
> But in the Roman activity as Cato, the entity was a writer of verse, a describer of those conditions which prompted the activities of the Romans in their surge through the varied lands, as well as the promptings of the activities of those in authority,

with little thought of the producer of those influences brought into the experiences of others—a
people to be ruled!

Thus we find, as the entity analyzes self and its
activities and its sojourns in the earth, there will be
found the abilities to write—whether as a reporter,
or of verse, or of prose, as a description of activities
of groups or sects or the like; these are of particular
interest to the entity.   2162-1

His past lives had provided him with innate talents
with both the arts and writing and in leading people. In
Jerusalem, [2162] had been a soldier and an architect. In
ancient Egypt he had been a builder of some of the
temples where he had gained the ability to direct others.

At the time of the reading, [2162] was a student at
Harvard. There are no additional follow-up reports as to
the direction the young man's life took.

Cecilia, Saint
ca. Second or Third Century
Case 2156

Considered the patron of music and musicians, Saint
Cecilia became a martyr for refusing to worship the Roman gods. One of the most famous saints of the early
church, she is revered for her virginity, for her conver-
sion of others to the faith, and for her distribution of pos-
sessions to the poor. According to legend, because of her
faith, Cecilia was ordered to be burned; however, the
flames could not harm her. As a result, she was beheaded.

The mother of a four-and-a-half-year-old daughter
obtained a life reading for her child. Others had commented that the young girl often appeared to be in touch
with something beyond the everyday world. Repeatedly,

she had been called a "wonder child" and a "little prophet." From the time the child had learned to speak, she had demonstrated an amazing psychic ability. In one instance, [2156] and her mother were sitting at the rear of a bus. The woman had just removed her daughter's leggings and overshoes and had convinced the girl to take a nap. Suddenly, the child jumped to her feet and demanded to have her winter attire put back on. The mother obliged and had no sooner finished when the whole rear end of the bus burst into flames. The bus was stopped in the midst of a heavy snowstorm, and everyone got out to safety. Cayce confirmed that the little girl was a very special soul:

Before this (in its sojourns) we find the entity was among those who were given a special service in the early activities of the Church, in the bringing of spiritual concepts into the minds of individuals through music.

Then the entity was Saint Cecilia—or as Celia the entity was first known, and then known for its abilities in the teaching and ministering to those in the various stages of man's expression and development there—in the Roman activity and experience of the early Church; for the entity brought hope, patience, understanding.

Thus we will find hours in the present oft when music—that is of the nature that brings into association those forces of the celestial as well as the mental and spiritual—will be the greater channel in which the entity may enable, or be enabled, to give the expressions of those messages, those lessons that will be so much a help, and bring hope, in the minds of others.   2156-1

According to the reading, the child's intuitive skills

came from her life as a prophetess. In ancient Egypt, she had developed great talents with music that could bring harmony into the lives of others. At the same time, she had learned to manifest spirituality through dance and rhythm, and had assisted women in preparing for child-birth. In the Holy Land, she had been a very spiritual woman and had therefore been able to give birth to a great spiritual leader. In the past she had also found beauty in "the music of the spheres, in the voice of nature itself." (2156-2)

Sensitive to the point of picking up on the thoughts of others, the child needed to be raised in as stable an environment as possible, her parents were advised. Her intuition could develop further to where it would eventually provide much assistance to humankind. Cayce also stated that [2156] could eventually become a great healer, both as a counselor and with the use of laying on of hands. The girl's parents were encouraged to give their child a musical outlet, which would assist her both mentally and spiritually.

Later, the girl's mother wrote that her husband was not at all supportive of their daughter's psychic ability and had done "everything under the sun to combat [it]." The parents later separated and the child went to live with her father, where she abandoned her psychic abilities. The last report on file, from 1960, states that [2156] had married and was living in Pennsylvania with her husband. At the time, both were involved in a wholesale distributing business.

Clay, Cassius Marcellus
1810-1903
Case 2162

Cassius Marcellus Clay was an American abolitionist, politician, and diplomat. The son of a slaveholder, he became a member of the Kentucky legislature but was defeated in 1841 because of his opposition to slavery. He established an anti-slavery publication, *True American,* later renamed *The Examiner.* He served as U.S. minister to Russia and helped to negotiate the purchase of Alaska in 1867. Shortly before his death, he was declared legally insane.

In 1940, a woman got a life reading as a birthday present for her son. The young man was told that his talents with writing and in working with people could be traced primarily to past lives he had lived as the American politician, Cassius Marcellus Clay, as well as the Roman poet, Valerius Cato. (See also "Cato, Valerius.")

Clay, Henry
1777-1852
Case 3155

In the decades prior to the Civil War, Henry Clay was known as one of the most influential political leaders in the United States. A champion of economic reform and development, he served in both the U.S. Senate and the House of Representatives and was secretary of state under President John Quincy Adams. Clay rose to fame as a master of political compromise and was instrumental in the creation of the Missouri Compromise (1820) and the Compromise of 1850, both of which resolved bitter disputes over the expansion of slavery.

A forty-eight-year-old financial advisor was told that he had often been instrumental in the affairs of human history. From a lifetime in ancient Rome, he had become a champion of freedom of speech and freedom of worship and possessed great talents as an orator. He had also served as a politician in several incarnations, including, what might be called, "Secretary of State" in ancient Persia. In ancient Egypt he had been an aid to the "common peoples," helping both individuals and groups solve their problems. According to his reading, his talents were, "In the field of politics, in the field of finance, in the field of helping endeavors in varied activities, the entity may find an outlet for its abilities. A good speaker, but speak truth—ever. A good persuader, but how persuadest thou? Temper these with mercy, with justice, with love, and may all be to the glory of God":

> For, we find that the entity was that figure known as Henry Clay, of whose character and activity so much has been written. Little need to be said here, as to whether there were developments or retardments. Well that the entity study the policies, the ideals, the characteristics of that entity, and in its own judgments *correct* those shortcomings—and especially as related to health; else these activities may be less efficient in a few years than they may be if precautions are taken.
>
> Use that ability of convincing others, as you attained through that experience, and all of the characteristics of the entity, rather to the glory of God and not to the glory of [3155].   3155-1

In 1954, [3155] requested another copy of his reading. After receiving it, he reported that the way his life reading had worked out was "quite a story in itself." However, the story was not reported. It is known that Mr. [3155] remained interested in the work of A.R.E. throughout his life.

Croesus
ca. 560 B.C.
Case 5001

Croesus is known as the last, and wealthiest, king of

Lydia. His fortune had been acquired through extensive trade with other countries. He conquered the Greeks of Ionia and was in turn conquered by the Persians. According to legend, he had a meeting with the Athenian lawgiver, Solon, who told the king that good fortune, not wealth, was the basis of all happiness. Reportedly, after being invaded by the Persians, rather than being assassinated, he received the lesser political office of governor.

In 1944, a thirty-two-year-old sheet metal worker received a life reading in which he was encouraged to overcome the innate urges that had caused him to abuse power over others. He was told that "no individual is worth much without a temper but he who cannot control it is worth much less." Among other inclinations that he had to meet and overcome in himself was his tendency to be controlling. Apparently, in one past life he had been a grower for a large plantation and had made certain his word was never questioned. He had also been the emperor Croesus, "a hard-hearted guy, with more power than he used properly":

> Before that the entity was in the Persian land as indicated, when the entity was then a king—one in authority—and one who abused authority. For with the repressions that came about through the activities of individuals warring in the desert, the entity was in the office and the activities of the second Croesus.
>
> The entity was among those who had power, wealth, fame, but abused most of these.
>
> Hence these ye meet in thy association, in thy companionship in the present, in the associations where there were turmoils and strifes.   5001-1

[5001] had also taken part in the Crusades, acting as a

guide to others. In that life he had "gained" and still possessed the ability to be helpful to individuals rather than controlling of them. Prior to that he had been a diplomat in ancient Egypt. Another tendency he had was to take himself too seriously.

Rather than suppressing his past associations with power and authority, he was advised to direct them into constructive channels where they could bring harmony into the lives of others. He was encouraged to put his trust in the authority of spirit rather than any man-made power.

Mr. [5001] was told that he had been married previously to his present wife—a woman from whom he was separated at the time of the reading—and that he should try to reconcile with her. Apparently, their marriage had failed previously and needed to be corrected: " . . . you made a mighty mess in the experience before this—ye suffered for it! Better make it up now or it'll be ten times worse the next time":

> Act toward the wife, or thine own activities, as ye would like her or others to act toward thee. Ask no more than ye give. Demand no more than ye allowed, or allow, to be demanded of thee. Marriage, such an association, is a oneness of purpose. Unless there is the oneness of purpose, there can be no harmony. This can be accomplished . . .

Other than the fact that [5001] and his wife later divorced and then married others, no additional reports are on file.

Cromwell, Oliver
1599-1658
Case 2903

A general, and lord protector of the Commonwealth, Oliver Cromwell became one of the most important figures in British history. Elected to Parliament in 1628, he was prominent in the English Civil War, which eventually led to the downfall of the monarchy. He pressed for the trial and execution of Charles I and would later rule England, Scotland, and Ireland under the Republican Commonwealth and Protectorate (1649-1658). He was among the first European leaders to proclaim religious toleration. A year after his death, the monarchy was reestablished, and in 1661 his corpse was disinterred, hanged, and beheaded by order of King Charles II.

A fifty-eight-year-old life insurance representative was told in 1925 that he had been Oliver Cromwell, as well as Xenophon, the Athenian historian and general. (See also "Xenophon.")

In the one before this, we find in that of him who gave the freedom to the peoples in the English rule, when the peoples rose and sought freedom from the yoke of the King. Then in the name, Oliver Cromwell, and the entity then fought for that principle in which there was then instilled in the inmost forces, and in the present we find that urge for the ability of each individual to find their place and to fill same in their best capacity, and in this also we find that desire ever is shown in the entity to give of the best, and not reserving self in any manner.

2903-1

The reading stated that he would have made a wonderful minister in the present. In other periods of development, [2903] had learned to put others first so that in the present anyone with whom he came in contact would benefit. He had been both counselor and historian to a ruler in ancient Egypt. During a lifetime in Peru, he had been second in command of the city. The reading said that he had innate abilities as a counselor and could instill faith and confidence in those around him, inspiring individuals to be of service. In a later reading, he was advised that he had problems with his eliminations, especially in the areas of the liver and kidney. When he died nearly twenty years later, the cause was listed as cirrhosis of the liver.

A relative later reported that during his life, [2903] had truly been "a grand man," possessing "magnetic attributes" which he had shared freely at home and in society.

Davis, Samuel
1843-1863
Case 391

Samuel Davis, a member of the Confederate army, was selected as a young recruit to scout for the South. In 1863, while carrying documents detailing Union troop activities, he was captured by Union soldiers. Despite repeated opportunities to cooperate, he refused to divulge the source of his information. The punishment was death. His last act before hanging was to write a note to his mother. A Sam Davis Monument, commemorating his gallantry, exists in Tennessee.

The sister of a sixteen-year-old boy requested a reading for her brother to help him decide on his life's work. The youth was told that he had been the Confederate War hero:

In the one before this we find the entity in that of

one in the same name as is given in the present time, and in that one acting as the messenger, or the informer, for certain division of soldiery, and suffered in the end for that held as honor to the entity. Then in the name Davis, and the entity gained through that experience, yet there is seen in the present urge that of the tendency of stubbornness, even to the entity's own undoing. Rather would the entity turn this into that way of applying self to the study *of* self, and not in as a grudge from others, for too easy does it (the condition) beget that which is as *not* of the mental, but of determination to rule or ruin!   391-1

From that same lifetime, he had a tendency toward stubbornness—a fault which would be repeatedly pointed out by others throughout his life. In a previous life, he had been a member of the expedition when Christopher Columbus had sailed to Puerto Rico. From that period, he had acquired the inclination to think of his own needs first whenever life got hard. In Greece he had been the director of games which had to do with physical prowess. For that reason, he possessed an innate urge to take part in sports. In Atlantis, he had been a counselor and gained a deep appreciation for that which was right and honorable in the lives of others.

He was encouraged to pursue a life's work that dealt with physical prowess and sports or to do something which would enable him to be a positive guiding force in the lives of others. Among other things, he was told that he also had an innate appreciation of flowers. After the reading, the young man thanked Mr. Cayce but explained that, "I don't like flowers so awfully much." Later, a physical reading would advise him to avoid alcoholic beverages.

Reportedly, [391] attempted to become a baseball

player but was never successful. Several stormy relationships and difficulties with alcohol would mark his life. He would be married three times. Throughout World War II, he traveled extensively and served in such places as Germany, Holland, and England, and for a time after the war, he would work in a wholesale flower business. He also held a number of jobs in restaurants and eating establishments. Later in his life he suffered from the effects of alcohol, tuberculosis, and emphysema—all of which would eventually kill him.

Elizabeth I
1533-1603
Case 2378

Considered one of England's greatest monarchs, Queen Elizabeth I is known for the age she inspired, as well as for the glamour of her court, her success as a ruler, and her long-preserved virginity. The Virginia colony was named for her. During her reign, England asserted itself as a power in politics, commerce, and the arts. She was the daughter of Henry VIII and his second wife, Anne Boleyn. Elizabeth was adept at foreign languages, loved music, and firmly established the Protestant Church of England during her reign.

During the course of her reading, a thirty-one-year-old woman asked why she often had "visions" of a revolving universe studded with stars. Cayce's response was that it symbolized the power which she had attained, for she had once "ruled the universe as the Queen!"

The entity was among those of the household of royalty, and in those experiences as the Queen Elizabeth made for those activities that were questioned by many, yet to many brought those periods of the greater consideration for the subjects of the land; the favors that were administered by the entity to those of various periods of activities in relationships to other lands brought many questionings.

As to whether or not it was a period of development, or of retardment, may be better determined by the manner in which the entity is *still* held in reverence by many of certain groups or classes in that particular land. And all of these should have a particular interest.   2378-1

In her most recent life, she had been born in colonial America from where she had gained a deep appreciation for soil, the outdoors, and the harmonies of nature. In Palestine she had experienced a great deal of turmoil because of religious prejudice and interference—a situation her soul had attempted to set right as the queen of England. She was affected by music and sound and also possessed an innate appreciation for color and tints. Each of these qualities was traced back as far as ancient Egypt when she had been employed in the temples and had excelled at music (especially the harp).

[2378] was told that she had high mental abilities, an innate attraction to nature and music, and could excel in any work that required detail, whether it was secretarial work or teaching music to others. She was warned of her tendency toward hardheadedness and was advised to look for work in "portions of Tidewater, Virginia." When Cayce was asked what her latent talent was, he replied that the "Greater expression may be found in those fields indicated. The latent talent, of course, is *ruling!* Hence the home is the better place to express it than in others, under the present environs."

No detailed follow-up reports for [2378] are on file.

Foster, Stephen
1826-1864
Case 5306

Although he was born in the North and never really liked the South, Stephen Foster was an American songwriter whose words and music have become associated with the American South. He began writing songs as a young boy and is known to have made only one trip to the South. Some of his best-known tunes include "My Old Kentucky Home" and "Camptown Races." In spite of the fact that he left behind approximately 200 songs, he never made much money. Stephen accepted a flat sum for each song, such as $100 for "O Susanna." Struggling with alcoholism and debt, he was left by his wife and died in virtual poverty.

In 1944, parents of a one-year-old boy had come to Edgar Cayce looking for guidance in directing their child's future. In beginning the reading, Cayce stated that this child—like so many others being born in the period between 1943 and 1946—was entering the earth with a definite purpose in mind. He went on to suggest that the focus and the future of the 1960s would be greatly dependent upon the activity of these very souls. The parents were told that their son's life would have a "tendency towards music" and that he should be directed in those educational possibilities that had to do with music, verse, and song:

> For the entity then was of the song writers whose words and music was of the type which has lived and will live longer than any one individual American.
>
> So, the entity will be so American as to be hard to get along with, even when other lands or names are mentioned, during the first twelve years of its sojourn in the earth.

For the entity was Stephen C. Foster, and how little others then thought of the entity and now how much he is thought of! but few, still, appreciate the abilities.

Hates will be easy for the entity, because of the slights and the slurs which were parts of the experience.

Evenness of temper will be those things to bring into the experience, through the gentleness, through the patience, manifested.   5306-1

Although the readings generally gave four or five past incarnations that were having an impact upon the present, in this case Cayce gave only one. The boy's parents were reminded of their tremendous responsibility in directing their son's education and future. They were told that additional past lives could be given for their information when the child was between the ages of ten and twelve and after they had attempted to bring some musical training into the boy's life.

No follow-up reports are on file.

Francis I
1494-1547
Case 2060

Francis I, king of France, is best known for having been ruler as France moved from the Middle Ages to the threshold of the modern era. He had almost no experience in state affairs when he ascended to the throne at the age of twenty-one, but he seemed suited for the role. He was a patron of the arts and a skilled military leader who led a number of important battles during his reign. Before his death, Francis would found a port at Le Havre, which eventually became a major seaport and an important commercial center for the country.

In 1939, the father of a twenty-four year old obtained a life reading for his son, [2060]. Eleven years previously, the young man had been given a physical reading for a bad cold. Although [2060] was now working as a clerk in a store, he was not satisfied with his job. In order to help his son, the father and a family friend requested a reading, "advising us as to his talents, ability, and what is the best work for him to follow for a successful life."

In beginning the reading, Cayce reminded [2060] and his father that each soul has many innate urges, abilities, and shortcomings, and that what an individual becomes in the present is dependent upon free will and what he or she chooses to do with life's opportunities:

> Before this the entity was that one known as Francis I of France; not considered (as may be seen from the records of history) as an altogether powerful or imposing ruler, and oft at variance to many of the activities about the entity in relationships to other lands.
>
> Hence things of a political nature have an attractiveness to the entity; abilities to direct the affairs of a community, a county, a state, a nation, have a great urge. And oft, in the reading or the hearing of an exposé upon the activities of anyone in authority, whether in its own land or in other lands, the entity finds self forming conclusions *immediately* as to what should have been, or should be in the present conditions, done as respecting same . . .
>
> It would be well, then, that the entity take that training which is desirable for preparation in the diplomatic service—rather than in the local political associations. Be above the petty politique, as the entity *attempted* to be in those activities through that particular sojourn.   2060-2

In addition to his lifetime as Francis I, [2060] was told that in Rome he had also been a merchant broker dealing with various countries and had developed abilities as a government representative and diplomat. Working with other cultures had also been a part of his lifetime in ancient Persia when he had been a banker involved in currency exchange among various kingdoms. During a lifetime in ancient Egypt, he had once again been a politician and diplomat. The reading made it clear that he had definite abilities in politics and working with others. He also had talents as a merchant, but Cayce suggested the young man would find a career as a merchant too limiting in exercising his abilities and it would become "a drag on the experiences, and abilities, of the entity."

A few years later, the young man's father stated that [2060] "has turned out a mighty fine fellow, very thoughtful and considerate." The last report on file states that [2060] had become an instructor in the air corps and was stationed at Kellogg Field in Battle Creek, Michigan.

Franklin, Benjamin
1706-1790
Case 165

One of the most admired men of the eighteenth century, Benjamin Franklin was known as a printer and publisher, author, inventor, and diplomat. He was one of seventeen children born into a pious, Puritanical family and began writing published essays at the age of sixteen. As a printer, he founded the *Pennsylvania Gazette* and *Poor Richard's Almanack* and established printing partnerships throughout the Colonies. By the time he began his diplomatic career, he had invented the lightning rod, bifocal spectacles, and the Franklin stove. While still in his forties, he had made a small fortune from his various business ventures. Involved in many activities, he

helped to found a fire company, a lending library, a college (which became the University of Pennsylvania), an
insurance company, a hospital, and a voluntary militia.
He helped draft the Declaration of Independence and
was instrumental in achieving the adoption of the U.S.
Constitution. Active all of his life, he spent his final years
promoting the abolition of slavery, his interest in philosophy, and the growth of the University of Pennsylvania.

In 1927, a fifty-year-old engineer, inventor, paint
manufacturer, and educator was told that he innately
possessed a great love of people, the pleasure of humor
and good wholesome fun, and the desire to bring greater
understanding into individuals' lives. His varied interests in business activities and the education of the young
was traced to the life just previously when he had been
Benjamin Franklin:

> In the appearances, and those urges seen from
> same:
> In the one before this we find during that period
> when much was being attempted in this present
> land. The entity then among those who builded for
> the good of those to come, ministering in many
> ways and in many manners to the needs of the na-
> tion yet unborn, and many of the words in verse, in
> line, are often yet quoted in schools, in places of
> learning, in copy. In the name then Franklin. The
> entity gained through this experience, giving self in
> *service* to many, rather than turning same into
> channels for self's own interest, as might have been
> done through that experience. In the urge is seen
> that of the love of the young, and of the making to-
> ward better manhood in the home, in the office, in
> the field.   165-2

His talent with government was traced to a life in Egypt when he had been a ruler and had developed the ability to "lead, guide, and direct" others. He also possessed abilities as a counselor and advisor. He was encouraged to remember the ideals of his past when he kept uppermost in his mind his deep love for people and when he often gave of himself for the enlightenment of others. At the same time, he was warned against pursuing selfish ventures or associations with others that were simply "for position, power, fame, or monies."

Mr. [165] believed that the life reading had pinpointed him extremely well and, as a result, he would become one of the most enthusiastic supporters of Cayce's work. In all, he would eventually obtain twenty-six readings on a variety of personal, physical, and business matters. In 1929, he joined with a group of others in attempting to create a pharmaceutical and health company that would provide individuals and hospitals with treatment regimens and therapies outlined in the Cayce readings. Unfortunately, two things appeared to destine the venture to failure from the beginning: one was the Depression, and the other was his adversarial relationship with Mr. [900], the chief financial backer of Cayce's Association. In the readings, the antagonism between the two was traced to previous lives in ancient Egypt and Israel when each had been on opposing sides. However, in spite of the fact that they were each reminded that they should now be working together, neither could resolve his mutual feelings of distrust and animosity, and thus their joint business dealings failed.

As long as he was able, [165] was a financial contributor to the Association; however, during the Depression he suffered great financial stress and lost his manufacturing firm. He supported himself and his family with various business activities, articles that he sold, and small engineering inventions. By 1938, he had become part of the hearing aid business and wrote that he was being in "close, intimate contact with individuals who are living in the silences. They need physical and spiritual help." However, his greatest love seemed to be in the direction of educating young people. As a result, he procured a number of readings on the establishment and creation of a school, which would help young men in their life's direction and vocation.

His interest in education continued until his sixty-third year when he was killed in an automobile accident.

Fritchie, Barbara
1766-1862
Case 2598

Barbara Fritchie became an American legend when, at the age of ninety, she defied the Confederate troops under Stonewall Jackson as they advanced through Frederick, Maryland. When the troops marched through town, she waved an American flag from her window and shouted, "Halt!" Reportedly, she told the Confederates that they could shoot her but that they needed to honor the country's flag. Although her boldness did not prevent the Confederate occupation, it did earn her a place in history. The story of her bravery became the subject of both a poem and a play.

In a life reading, Cayce told a sixty-four-year-old woman that she had once been Barbara Fritchie. Born fifteen years after Fritchie's death, [2598] was an actress who was frustrated that her career had never really gotten off the ground. Cayce began the reading by noting that [2598] was "a beautiful person!":

> In writing may the entity accomplish the most in this present experience. The abilities are in any field as would have to do, or in dealing with others,

groups, masses, *as* a lecturer; but preferably as a writer . . .

Then, with that will that knows no defeat, the entity may accomplish here and now, in this experience, much that seemingly has just escaped the entity in its ability to make contacts or to get the proverbial "break" in its associations and activities . . .

Before this the entity was in the land of the entity's present sojourn . . . in the name Barbara Frietchie [Fritchie].   2598-2

The woman's interest in acting and the theater was traced to several previous incarnations. During the Greco-Roman period, she had been a male actor bringing to the Roman world knowledge and experiences through drama and voice. From this same experience, she also possessed an innate ability in writing. From an Egyptian life, she possessed abilities as both a writer and artist. She was told, "Thus the entity has been and is a good dancer, a good musician, a good artist. There is very little of the arts with which the entity is not familiar." More than anything, she was encouraged to pursue work in writing.

When she asked why she was having such a difficult time pursuing her acting, she was told not to think of it as a hardship but rather as a means of enabling her to manifest her innate abilities as a writer. Again, she was encouraged to "*Do* write. *Do* talk. *Do* so live as to never condemn thyself, and to the glory of Him who is the way, the truth, the light."

Later, [2598] wrote to confirm that she had investigated the life of Barbara Fritchie and the two had a number of things in common. In addition to having been born in Maryland of German descent and possessing an innate call to "doing one's duty," there was a great love for nature and for growing things. [2598] owned some property which she called "Little Paradise" and had a strong belief in the reality of nature sprites, fairies, and devas.

In spite of the readings' suggestion that she pursue writing and speaking, [2598] continued to feel that acting was her calling. She later wrote, "I want the stage more than anything in the world." She claimed to have no real affinity for writing and yet Gladys Davis, Edgar Cayce's secretary, would later note that [2598] had written "voluminous" amounts of correspondence detailing her feelings and her life's events. In fact, [2598]'s correspondence is greater than many of the individuals who had readings from Edgar Cayce.

Mrs. [2598] remained an active supporter of Cayce's work until she passed away in 1949.

Gladstone, Sir Edmund William
1809-1898
Case 3340

Gladstone is considered the greatest British statesman of the nineteenth century. Born as the son of a Liverpool merchant, he was in Parliament for over sixty years and served as prime minister four times. Although he began his career as a conservative, he became a driving force behind social and political reform. A member of the Anglican Church, he always sought to apply morality to politics. While in government, he served as president of the Board of Trade. During his time in office, he was known for his tax reforms and tried, unsuccessfully, to abolish the income tax. He secured an important commercial treaty with France and campaigned to put an end to Britain's colonial expansion. In an attempt to solve the ongoing conflict between Britain and Ireland, he advocated giving the Irish Home Rule, an effort which split the Liberal party and failed to win the support it needed.

A noted attorney was told that he had attracted the soul of William Gladstone to be his son because of the man's interest in Gladstone as well as his study of British history. The boy had come into the family through adoption and had been named William. Cayce advised that the child had the opportunity to do something about international relationships as well as the political economy:

> For, before this the entity was known as the "grand old man" of England—William Gladstone— that directed through a period of the activities there, the affairs of the land as they had never before been directed. And those influences are yet to bear fruit for the English people as well as much of another source of karma from others that have been in the place of power. Too much has been said for other than the comment which has been indicated for the direction.   3340-1

His parents were advised to direct their child in law, economics, and international relationships. It was even possible that the boy could become secretary of state. He had served Nero and had attempted to placate persecutions and bigotry. He had gained abilities with exchange rates and international currency during a lifetime in Persia and had functioned as an emissary in ancient Egypt.

In spite of the fact that the boy's parents maintained a lifetime interest in the Cayce work, few reports are on file. In 1998, the boy's stepmother stated that [3340] had a difficult time in school and had chosen a career as a CPA rather than that of a lawyer. After almost twenty years as a CPA, he had turned instead to the insurance business. Great with people, she stated that [3340] was "one of the most loving individuals" she had ever met.

Gosse, Edmund
1849-1928
Case 4035

English poet and critic, Gosse was born in London and educated privately. He is most known for his autobiographical work, *Father and Son,* in which he details his relationship with his father, Philip Henry Gosse, the naturalist. The author of numerous volumes of literary criticism, he introduced the works of a number of Scandinavian authors (such as Ibsen) to the English-speaking world. For his achievements, he was knighted in 1925.

In 1944, a twenty-seven-year-old army lieutenant* requested a life reading after finishing Cayce's biography, *There Is a River.* He was confused as to his life's direction and his apparent apathy for the activities and the people in his life. In addition to his army career, he professed a great love for languages and literature. The reading advised him that his life just previous to the present "isn't all pretty." Apparently, the lieutenant had once been a writer and "a critic":

> For the activities of the entity in the experience before this, as Edmund Grosse [Gosse?] were, as a critic, and these bring doubts and fears. For as one sows, so must he also reap . . . When there is the attempt to use thy abilities, use them in a just cause and in a purposefulness; having something to say

*Note: Since [4035] was born in 1916 and Edmund Gosse died in 1928, we have to assume one of several possibilities: (1) Edgar Cayce made a mistake; (2) Gladys Davis, Cayce's secretary, made a mistake when taking down the name; (3) there was, in fact, an "Edmund Grosse" of which we have no historical data; or (4) although unusual, simultaneous incarnations may somehow be possible.

that is to the entity itself first not merely idealistic but a constructive ideal, whether it be pertaining to that of a historical nature, political nature, economic nature or pertaining to a purposeful correlation of activities or ideals of nations or groups of nations, or whether pertaining to sectionalism in a state or a nation. All of this has been and may yet be a part of the experience of the entity in its activity in the present.   4035-1

During the course of the reading, Cayce warned [4035], "As ye have criticized, know that ye thyself must be criticized." Rather than being all bad, his lifetime as Gosse had also nurtured his abilities as a writer. These same abilities were present and could be further cultivated in [4035]'s life. He was encouraged to pursue writing in the direction of prose, fiction, or history. Cayce added:

To be sure, as in any line of endeavor, to succeed as a writer one must write; though the entity might attempt such for a year or more and never go farther than reading same and tearing it up, keep at it! For ye may accomplish much, even in the one best seller; that is, if thy purpose is set correctly for that which should be or would be written. Have thy ideals set as for that which is ever constructive; not merely for thy ability as a dramatic critic.

Previous lives had also included being an emissary for the Romans, from which he had acquired a love of the history of people; he had served as a record-keeper for the Israelites; and in ancient Egypt he had been, what might be termed, a historian. [4035] was reminded to not pass judgment or condemn anyone and to pursue his talents in record-keeping and writing. He was also told that his present girlfriend had been his companion in

Egypt, and that they could continue a relationship as long as they held in mind what they had in common.

There are no follow-up reports on file.

Hamilton, Alexander
1757-1804
Case 142

Considered one of the most influential Founding Fathers of the United States, Alexander Hamilton led a remarkable life. His political career, however, was cut short in 1804 when he was killed in a duel with his rival, Aaron Burr. Born an illegitimate child, he displayed great military skill which brought him to the attention of George Washington. After the Revolutionary War, Hamilton studied law and became active in politics. Together with John Jay and James Madison, he wrote *The Federalist* papers, which helped shape American politics. As the country's first secretary of the treasury, he was responsible for placing the new nation on firm financial footing and for creating the Bank of the United States. More so than many of his contemporaries, Hamilton was a champion of a strong centralized national government.

Married for two years, a young Jewish couple were delighted to find that they were expecting a child. By all accounts the father was a financial genius and had made a fortune on Wall Street. The mother had several dreams during the pregnancy about her forthcoming child. In one, she dreamed that she had given birth to a fair, blue-eyed child, but in another she dreamed that the boy was "weak-minded."

In response to the mother's query about the second dream, Cayce stated that although it was true that before a potential condition became a reality it was often first dreamed, primarily her dream was regarding her unborn child's inclination toward emotional immaturity.

Cayce told her that when rearing the boy, she needed to keep in mind the biblical statement, "When I was a child I thought as a child. Now I become a man I put away childish thoughts." Apparently, the soul had never outgrown certain childish behaviors. After the birth of their son, the readings stated that these tendencies principally "have to do with those conditions regarding temper and the exercising of same as regards the will's influence." Their child had been Alexander Hamilton:

As to the appearances and influences as urges that will be presented in this entity:

In the one before this the entity was in that known as Hamilton [Alexander Hamilton], who presented the financial conditions to this present generation and peoples, and who in honor served mankind; in self's own personal interest lost in expression of defense of honor of that position held.

The urge seen in the present experience will be the exceptional interest in the financial conditions of those with whom the entity may be associated and of the mental study of those conditions related to same.   142-1

As in many families, the child had past lives with both parents and had purposefully chosen them in the present. In Troy, the child had gone to war in defense of Helen of Troy [136], the child's present mother. (See also "Helen of Troy.") From that period, [142] had cultivated a tremendous love for his mother. From a lifetime in Israel, the entity had been a scribe in service to the Temple. From that period came an interest in laws as well as the Jewish religion. He was also a scribe in ancient Egypt and a soldier at the same time his father had once been a soldier; and he had been a financier when his father was a theologian.

Rather than going into great detail about the child's abilities, Cayce stated that they would build and unfold based upon [142]'s direction in the present. His future would be dependent upon his education and training. The parents were encouraged to be a helpful influence in the child's rearing, especially during the first twelve years of his upbringing. Once again, they were reminded of the importance of helping their son control his temper. The boy had chosen them both because each could be helpful in his growth and development.

Unfortunately, when the boy was still only a few years old, his father became interested in another woman, causing the boy's mother to leave and obtain a divorce. In 1933, a family friend wrote that the divorce had prompted [142]'s mother to start "drinking like a fish!" With the Depression, the boy's father ended up losing his fortune, causing him to take [142] out of private schools. As a result, he went to live with his mother who got full custody. Afterward, he never remembered seeing his father. Nothing was heard about the child until he was a young man.

In 1952, a friend of the young man's mother wrote that she had seen him (he was then twenty-five) and found him to be good-looking: "At first we liked him, but as the evening wore on he showed a very dogmatic attitude about life in general. It has not been easy and I'm afraid there are scars . . . He had one-and-one-half years in the navy—spent three years at the University of Louisiana and decided to join his mother in N.Y. He is working with a wholesale jewelry house. [His mother] is anxious to see him married . . . "

In 1953, word was received that [142] had been sent to a psychiatric hospital for shock treatments because of an episode with his violent temper. In spite of the situation, the doctor gave a good prognosis and [142] was released within a few months. The next year, he visited

A.R.E. to obtain copies of the life readings for himself and his mother. His father had died that year, and [142] expressed regret that he had never attempted to reconcile before his father's death. At the time, [142] said that he had decided to make application to become a rabbi. No additional reports are on file.

Hancock, John
1737-1793
Case 4228

John Hancock was a Massachusetts merchant who achieved prominence as a member and president of the Second Continental Congress. He was the wealthiest merchant in Boston, and his interest in colonial independence was groomed by Samuel Adams. He became the first to sign the Declaration of Independence. He had a great deal of ambition and was disappointed when George Washington was chosen commander-in-chief of the army. In addition to his statesmanship, Hancock was known for his vanity and great love of popularity. As governor of Massachusetts, he was instrumental in getting his state to ratify the U.S. Constitution.

In 1923, the father of a six-year-old boy requested a horoscope reading (later called a life reading) for his son. It is interesting to note that the boy's father was the first individual to request a life reading for himself, [5717]. As the readings always did for young people, Cayce reminded the boy's parents of their important role in raising their son. They were told that the boy was given to "high exalted positions of self," that he was strong in body and mind, and that he would begin to hold positions of power even at the age of twenty-one. In later life, he would become interested in the sciences, but early on it would be politics that called to him:

One whose force and vocation will lie in that of letters, state papers, state organization, state direction, for this has been, as we see, an early return from those forces when last upon this plane . . .

In those of appearances, we find as these:

Before this in the courts of the present plane and sphere, and was the first signer of the declaration of these peoples here, this sphere here. This shows in the characteristics of the present entity. That of the greater show of self, and self principles—J O H N H A N C O C K, John Hancock.   4228-1

The parents were also told of earlier lives in England, Persia, and Atlantis when their son had developed his intuition, his ability with government, and his interest in chemical forces.

Although a file notation from 1952 states that [4228]'s father frequently bragged about the accuracy of his son's reading, no detailed information is on file.

Harvey, William
1578-1657
Case 2892

William Harvey is considered the founder of modern physiology. He was an English anatomist and physician who theorized and confirmed the way in which blood circulates in the human body. His work explained the function of the heart as a pump. He was also a court physician to King Charles I, who was a patron of Harvey's research. Harvey's experiments were published in *On the Motions of the Heart and Blood,* which became a classic in the field of science.

A mother requested a life reading for her five-month-old son in order to obtain guidance in rearing her child. During the course of the reading, Cayce stated that the

boy would have a great imagination, he would be extremely intelligent, determined to the point of stubbornness, and he would insist on "wanting to have his own
way, and knowing a little bit better just how to do things
than anyone else!" The child was destined to be a professional man "in the fields as of medicine, or dentistry,
or as a pharmacist. *Any* of these will be channels through
which the entity may attain nearer the fulfilling of those
purposes":

> We will find in Jupiter, as the unfoldments come,
> the greater universal consciousness, giving the
> abilities which *were* expressed by the entity in an
> experience as toward things and conditions associ-
> ated with the anatomical structure of an individual.
> For, the entity was Harvey—Dr. Harvey, discoverer
> of the circulation, and knew more about it than any-
> one else! Though proven to be in error in many
> things, he still insisted he knew the best! The activi-
> ties of that entity are well known, and if studied will
> give those responsible for the entity an idea as to
> the problems to be met.
> But *do* give the entity those opportunities of
> study, especially in that field either as a pharmacist
> or as a dentist, and he will do the rest himself as he
> goes along with these activities!   2892-2

During a life in France, the soul had also made discov-
eries regarding the relationship between cleanliness and
the catching of disease. This caused [2892] to have a fe-
tish about personal cleanliness. During the Greco-Roman period he had been involved with entertainment
and dance for the nobility, which had given him an ability to be sociable with others. In ancient Egypt he had
helped others with vocational guidance. In that same
lifetime he had grown very close to his present-day

mother. Finally, the parents were told that twice previously (in France and in Egypt) he had been in opposition with his present-day father; for that reason, there would be "a good many spats between 'em!"

During the boy's tenth year, his mother noted:

[2892] has shown particular interest in the physical body since a tiny child, and especially anything having to do with the heart and the circulation of the blood. He also definitely has the trait of insisting he is right. He never wants to admit that another's explanation of anything is better than his. Has been an A-1 student, boasts of having had better grades than anyone in school. Has a mind that researches into knowledge along whatever line he gets started. Has a phobia about germs—washes his hands all the time—definitely "hipped" on the subject. Doesn't want to live in a big city because of "all those people breathing germs on you" . . . Although we have never discussed his reading with him, he insists he's going to be a doctor. Has a paper route (at ten years old) and is saving money towards college.

The boy also loved nature and frequently studied all kinds of plant life. A later notation stated that "'spats' with his father were especially true through his teens." The mother added, "In fact, I can't think of a single instance where the reading was not exactly right."

The last report on file was in 1963 when [2892] was twenty:

He is doing splendidly in every way. His greatest interests seem to be in science studies, especially biology (botany, genetics, etc.). He has not yet decided (in his second year of college) on his major; perhaps he will teach, he says.

Hector
ca. Twelfth Century B.C.
Case 5717

According to Greek mythology, Hector, the son of the Trojan king, led his people's forces in the Trojan War. He is a central character of Homer's *Iliad* and is depicted as the noblest hero. In the tenth year of the war, he was killed by Achilles. After his death, he was buried with great honor, and his life was celebrated with nine days of mourning.

In 1923, in a reading tracing the historical relationships of four individuals, Cayce briefly stated that one of the men [5717] had been Hector and the four had each taken part in the Trojan War. They were encouraged to work together in the present. Interestingly enough, in 1933 Edgar Cayce had a dream that seemed to confirm the identity of [5717] as Hector:

> . . . I was a man, and among those guarding the gates . . . I saw all the fighting, being a guard at the gate . . . I wore a garment that would be called something of a toga today. My trousers were composed of a cloth wrapped around me, gathered and pinned in the middle between my legs. Then another square piece of cloth with a hole for my head dropped over my shoulders. I made armholes in this piece, so that my arms could come through and not have to throw the garment out of the way; which method was afterward adopted by most of the army (or the people, for I didn't recognize them as an army). I saw the battle between Hector and Achilles, recognizing these two as the individuals I now know as [5717] and [900]. They were both beautiful of countenance. Both had matted black ringlets on their heads, which reminded me of Medusa. The

hair seemed to be their strength. I noticed that Achilles was very hairy, while Hector only had hair on his neck—which was a different color from the hair on his head. I saw Hector dragged through the gate which I was guarding, into a large arena; and was dragged around the arena several times. Although he was losing, and had lost, quite a bit of blood—leaving the ground and stones bloody as he was dragged along, I noticed that he hadn't wholly lost consciousness. Eventually, the horses—in turning very swiftly, with Achilles driving—caused Hector's head to be dashed against the pillar or the gate near me, and his brains ran out. Before he had even lost the life, or the quiver of the muscles and nerves, I saw the carrion birds eat the great portions of his brain.   294-161

Helen of Troy
ca. Twelfth Century B.C.
Case 136

In Greek mythology, Helen of Troy was known as the most beautiful woman in the world and the indirect cause of the Trojan War. Because of her beauty, she was sought by every prince in Greece, but she finally married Menelaus, king of Sparta. She was abducted by Paris to Troy, causing ten years of fighting for her return. After Troy's defeat, Helen was returned to her husband. In older age, she was driven out of the kingdom by her step-sons and she fled to Rhodes. There, she was hanged by the queen in retaliation for the Trojan War.

In 1925, a twenty-year-old woman was referred for a reading by her boyfriend (who would later become her husband). The reading stated that she had been Helen of Troy. It is interesting to note that her boyfriend was told that he had once been Achilles. (See also "Achilles.")

In the one before this we find during the days
when the Trojan forces were being attacked, the
entity was in that capacity of one whom there was
much made over, being in that of Helen of Troy. The
entity then was in that development in the higher
forces as found in physical body, development in
mind, development in the law of love. In the present
earth's plane we find the abilities to bring about self
those who seek to give the acknowledgment of the
abilities of the entity to fascinate many. Not in the
manner of the one seeking those of the nature, yet
the innate ability to bring these conditions; yet
never lording them over any.   136-1

Miss [136] was told that she was sentimental, and matters of love were extremely important to her. Although
she was slow to anger, she was "one who holds [a] grudge
when once aroused." She was advised to try to work
through this soul inclination. In previous lives, she had
been an attendant to the wife of Charles I; and although
she had developed skills as a counselor from that incarnation, she also had learned how "to get even." She had
been a musician in ancient Egypt during a lifetime in
which she had made great spiritual progress.

She was told to direct her energies into the building of
a home "on a firm foundation" and the raising of a family. She could be extremely helpful to others in this regard. (See also "Hamilton, Alexander," [142], her son.)
Although she had not known her soon-to-be-husband
in Troy, he had known her from afar. The two had been
together in Egypt. Because she had a soul tendency to
wish to dominate those around her, she was advised to
seek the harmony with others she had once found in
Egypt.

Unfortunately, several years after [136] and her boyfriend [900] married and had a son, [900] expressed an

interest in another woman. The result was that [136] left her husband, obtained a divorce, and got full custody of their son, [142]. In the 1950s, a family acquaintance noted that if [136] hadn't possessed the innate tendencies of holding a grudge and desiring to get even, the marriage might have been saved, and the lives of her, her husband, and her son might have turned out very differently.

Henry, Patrick
1736-1799
Case 2294

Patrick Henry came to prominence as the most brilliant orator of the American Revolution. His ability to speak and inspire an audience gave him a tremendous influence in the legislature. In an impassioned call to the Colonies to arm themselves against British rule he pleaded, "Give me liberty, or give me death." He became governor of Virginia and for a time was an ardent supporter of state's rights versus a strong centralized government. Just prior to his death, however, he became a member of the Federalist party.

Without success, a couple had tried "everything" in order to conceive a child. As a last resort, they had gone to Edgar Cayce for a reading. Because of the physical reading and the suggestions that Cayce provided, the woman was able to get pregnant. The couple was delighted with the birth of their son, and when he was only one month old, they obtained a life reading for the boy.

Edgar Cayce began the reading by telling the parents that they "Should have named him Patrick!" As was always the case, the reading stated that it was providing that information which would be most helpful to the individual in fulfilling his purpose in the present. Cayce advised that there could be some difficulty with the child's health and that the boy should receive another reading at the age of twelve which could provide further advice as to the boy's upbringing. The child had an innate inclination toward extravagance and would make (and spend) a great deal of money. An excellent orator, [2294] would "always want to 'argue out' everything."

In a life in Rome, the boy had been a famous poet, historian, and senator, where he had excelled at being able to express the ideals and desires of the common people. (See also "Tacitus, Cornelius.") In Persia, he had been involved in trade and merchant caravans, from where he had gained a love of travel. In ancient Egypt, he had become extremely adept at working with various emissaries from different lands. Portions of the reading are as follows:

> ... in the developing years, there will be the tendency to seek liberty for its own self at any cost; and there should be given the whys, the causes, and the expression of the abilities that are reached through the Mercurian high mental experience ...
>
> As to the appearances of the entity in the earth, then:
>
> Before this the entity was in the land of the present nativity, as we have indicated, and one whose general activities are well known—in the name then Patrick Henry ...
>
> Hence the entity should be trained in *international law,* rather than local; for the opportunities and the needs for such are to be a part of the entity's experience ...
>
> Much in this experience, as indicated, will depend upon the manner of the training as to activities in the early portion of the entity's sojourn here. Hence the responsibilities lie mostly with and upon those to whom the entity has been entrusted.
>
> 2294-1

No detailed follow-up reports are on file for [2294].

James V
1512-1542
Case 1378

James was only seventeen months old when he succeeded to the throne of Scotland. During the first half of his reign, while still a child, he was used as a pawn in the struggle between pro-English and pro-French factions. When he gained control of his rule, he allied with France and upheld Roman Catholicism against Protestantism. Because of his defeat in a struggle with the army of his uncle, King Henry VIII, he suffered a mental breakdown and later died.

In 1937, a woman requested a life reading for her critically ill father, [1378]. She stated, "There is, and always has been, a deep bond of sympathy and understanding between us. When I was a child he used to talk to me of reincarnation and the like, and in those days it was not much thought of, or discussed. He had a brilliant mind and college education, but liquor got the best years of his life, until recent years. But I can only pity him, because I know he had a good kind heart, and there is a reason for everything."

The reading was given and stated:

For the entity (as all) is constantly meeting self . . . God looketh on the heart while man looketh on the outward appearances.

As to the experiences in the earth:

Much of that which is a matter of record as to the entity's activity in the experience before this is manifested in a different circumstance in the present experience. The likes and dislikes for individuals' activity; those particulars that have to do with the minutest detail—as of certain names, conditions that pertain to royalty, position, and conditions that pertain to freedom of speech, freedom of church, freedom of physical activity.

Then the entity was in the name, as called, James V of England (Scotland); and those experiences have been recorded—both pro and con. Thus there is little need of the interpreting of same, in the light of that which has just been indicated.   1378-1

Previously, [1378] had been an elder in the Sanhedrin, one who frequently questioned the Scriptures. In the same lifetime, he would eventually befriend and support a number of the apostles. In addition to his interest in spirituality, he had developed the innate tendency to be a "stickler for details." In Persia, he had been advisor to the king, often providing the ruler with effective counsel. In ancient Egypt, he had served in the same capacity.

Mr. [1378] was reminded that life was a continuous experience and that even death only brought a "change" in one's state of consciousness. He was encouraged to put his trust in God.

According to [1378]'s daughter, her father died shortly after receiving the reading. She was extremely grateful that they had obtained it in time. She stated, "I don't think that anything in this life has made me more happy." She felt that the reading had been of great comfort, sparing her a great deal of sorrow.

Jay, John
1745-1829
Case 1188

John Jay was one of the leading political figures during the American Revolution. He sought stability in the new nation and favored continued close ties with Britain. He served the U.S. as a diplomat to both Spain and France. One of the authors of *The Federalist* papers, he favored a strong national government sympathetic to industry and commerce. George Washington appointed him the first chief justice of the U.S. Supreme Court, a role in which he created procedures that remain in effect to this day. He resigned from the Supreme Court and served as governor of New York. Perhaps because he lost public favor as a result of a trade agreement negotiated with Great Britain, he refused further public office and retired to his farm for the remaining twenty-seven years of his life.

One of the stories associated with John Jay is the following: He and some colleagues stopped at a tavern somewhere between Philadelphia and Washington. The handmaid who waited on their table was extremely beautiful and Jay allegedly commented that the color of the girl's face resembled the beauty of a conch shell. The four men agreed not to tell anyone of the location of this beautiful woman, reportedly so they could keep her to themselves. This tale was repeatedly retold with a great deal of humor for years thereafter. What is remarkable about this story is the fact that when [1188] was four years old, he was walking along the beach with his nanny/nurse when he stopped to pick up a pink conch shell. In later years, he recalled:

I connected that conch shell with something so foreign to my present life that I momentarily forgot who I was or where I was. This annoyed the nurse and it was she who brought me out of my vagary. It took me a moment to adjust myself but when I did I was startled at the speed with which I forgot the details of my recent contemplation. I do remember that I turned to the nurse and asked her if people's faces are ever the color of conch shells. She seemed very bored with the question which annoyed me considerably because I felt at the time that I had experienced something unusual and that I had good reason for asking the question.

When the boy was six, his connection with Jay was confirmed. Because of [1188]'s connection with John Jay, it is interesting to note that the child was born in Bronxville, New York, while the rest of his family was from Ohio:

> Hence as we find, law—especially trained in that phase of same where activities would deal with machinery or corporations that deal in same; or of railroads or of airways or machinery of that nature—would become a portion of the entity's *natural* inclinations . . .
>
> The entity then, in the name of John Jay, made a study of national and international relationships, as pertained to laws of the various effects of individuals and groups and their abilities to be considered as individuals and groups in combination with a nation's activity. These throughout the experience made for manifestations in the activity of the entity, and the entity gained throughout.   1188-3

The boy's reading stated that he was affectionate, sentimental, and prone to "worry over trifles." A previous life in the Holy Land had developed interests in spirituality and philosophy. In Chaldea he had been a general during the time of Alexander the Great. From that same period, he had developed an intense interest in things of a mechanical nature. In Egypt, he had been a counselor to the king. As far as his talents were concerned, he would be good at debate, but that ability might be overshadowed by his interest "in those things of a mechanical or machine nature."

As a young man, he joined the ROTC and served as a lieutenant in the army. All through school and the army he had a deep interest in philosophy, the work of Edgar Cayce, and political science. In the 1950s he took a job with an airplane company in the Northwest. At the time, he still hoped to take a correspondence course in law. He found frequent occasions to debate philosophy and reincarnation with those of a more fundamentalist background. The last report on file is a Christmas card from 1963 when [1188] stated that he was still an employee of the same company and "I suspect that the chance is better than even that I will remain in the Northwest."

Jefferson, Thomas
1743-1826
Case 1208

Thomas Jefferson was the third president of the United States, but he wished to be remembered chiefly for three things, according to the inscription he wrote for his tombstone: that he was "author of the Declaration of American Independence, of the Statute of Virginia for religious freedom, and Father of the University of Virginia," and—as Jefferson insisted—"not a word more."

In addition to his presidency and the statements of his epitaph, Jefferson was the first secretary of state and an influential political leader and philosopher. He also served as governor of Virginia. In 1803, during his presidency, he acquired the Louisiana Purchase for the United States, greatly increasing the size of the country. At his advice, the United States adopted the dollar and the decimal system for the nation's monetary unit, rather than the pound. Although a slave owner himself, Jefferson believed it was an evil that shouldn't be allowed to spread. He fought against the expansion of slavery beyond the original thirteen colonies, but was defeated. After his retirement from public office in 1809, Jefferson spent his remaining years engaged in the establishment of the University of Virginia. He had talents as an architect and an inventor and possessed a wide range of knowledge and appreciation of the arts and sciences.

In 1936, Cayce told the parents of a two-day-old boy that if their son was raised properly he would have a tremendous impact upon the world. Apparently, the soul had been two very influential figures from the past: Thomas Jefferson and Alexander the Great. (See also "Alexander the Great.")

> For, as the entity in its relationships must belong as it were to the *world,* it will regard all peoples alike. For those influences and activities will be the greater influence, if those directions are made in the experiences of its development as to its proper relationships and choices as to its associations.
>
> For the high and the low, those of fame and those of defame, will be *as one* to the entity without reason—unless guided aright . . .
>
> As to the appearances in the earth and those that influence the entity in the present—if there are the activities directed or guided as has been indicated in its sojourn in the early portion, or the formative years, in the choice of the entity:
>
> Before this, as given, the entity lived in the earth during those periods when there were the turmoils in that known as the Revolution, and in the activities of the Colonists.
>
> The entity then, as Thomas Jefferson, made these contributions to the activities of the people—that are well known, or may be had through the many

references that may be drawn upon [by] those seeking to know.   1208-1

Although he had gained as a soul in his lifetime as
Jefferson, as Alexander the Great [1208] had come to be-
lieve that power made for right and he had acquired a
tendency toward personal indulgence. That trait, if not
curbed in the present, would run wild and lead to his
downfall. In terms of pinpointing the boy's talents in the
present, Cayce stated that that was problematical because it was greatly dependent upon the parents and the
child's upbringing. In fact, at least seven times in [1208]'s
reading, Cayce reminded them of their important role in
guiding and directing this child.

More so than many, this case has a great deal of com-
munication and reports on file. In spite of Cayce's advice, the boy's parents gave their child a very rocky
upbringing. They would separate and reconcile many
times during his formative years, moving the boy from
one location to another. Eventually the boy's parents
would divorce and [1208] would spend a number of
years living with his aunt rather than either parent. His
teenage years were difficult and, at seventeen, he ran
away with a friend to Florida where the two got into
trouble for stealing. Beginning in 1955, he would serve a
stint in the marine corps.

After the marine corps, he spent time in what his aunt
called a "Bohemian type of life." He would try careers in
sales, music, and the clothing business. He would marry
and divorce several times, all the while trying to "get hold
of myself." His travels would take him to places like Japan, Greece, Italy, Spain, and Africa. It was apparent to
his friends and family that he had many talents, but
much of his life seemed spent in trying to find himself.

Joan of Arc, Saint
ca. 1412-1431
Case 302

Joan of Arc is considered the greatest national heroine of France. When she was about thirteen years old, she claimed to have begun hearing voices of saints which gave her the mission of liberating France from English domination. Although a peasant girl and only seventeen years old, she revived the hopes of French troops during the Hundred Years' War by leading them to victory against the English. Afterward, she was condemned as a heretic by the English-dominated French church for refusing to deny her claim to divine inspiration. As a result, she was burned at the stake. Her conviction was later overturned and she was canonized in 1920.

A thirty-six-year-old saleswoman employed at a stock brokerage firm obtained a series of readings from Edgar Cayce. She was extremely interested in dreams and had several dream interpretation readings. She also requested several readings about a love affair she wished to pursue. Repeatedly, Cayce advised against it and [302] later admitted that she could have avoided much suffering if she had followed his advice. In her life reading, she was told that she had an innate power over men which could be used "for weal or woe." In the past she had been Joan of Arc:

One that has the ability to destroy or to make men.
One that has the ability to be at ease in an office, whether of men, among men, or in the drawing room of the elite, or one that is in a sick room, or in the pleasure hall—or the ability to adapt self to that position, condition, in which the entity finds self . . .

In the one before this we find in that period in the French rule when the woman rose to the position of the leader in that land. The entity then in that of the leader, and becoming—as has been seen, made, in the minds of many—the criterion for strength and for beauty. Yet persecuted in that day, and in all gaining and losing—gaining and losing. In the name—Joan of Arc. The entity then in that of the present experience finds that desire to lead, to guide, to direct—yet, as is seen, the power of the abilities seems ever not *just* in the *right* direction.

302-1

Her reading stated that in Troy she had been the mother of Achilles, [900], her present employer. She had lost in that lifetime due to her misuse of power and position. She had been leader of her land during a lifetime in Egypt. She was told that her greatest talent was as "a leader, instructor, teacher, or director" and yet she must first balance herself, remembering that the soul's greatest desire was to be at-one with the Creative Forces. Finally, she was encouraged to "Keep thy paths straight."

Her employer wrote to confirm the fact that she had great abilities in directing others and that she had been extremely helpful to the firm. Unfortunately, he felt that she didn't have a clear understanding of her abilities and sometimes used them (and her sexuality) for control over others:

She oscillates back and forth even as she does with her power, seeing no other way of using it than to make people bring her material success. If she could only see the further greater use of it—how wonderful to lift people up who are bowed down with grief, sickness, misfortune and cares and inspire them to fight their way to better conditions

. . . What a wonderful opportunity she, [302], has if she only awakens in time . . . She of her own free will must choose, and as she chooses so will her life become merited beauty, love, and happiness, or that which has no more value than the few living on earth today may measure in terms of dollars.

For a time, she proved extremely helpful to the work of Cayce's Association; however, a routine mailing in 1938 was returned address unknown. No additional reports are on file.

Kidd, Captain (William)
ca. 1645-1701
Case 2213

Captain Kidd became romanticized as a legendary seventeenth-century pirate in fictional literature. Historically, it is believed that William Kidd went to sea as a youth, where he grew to become a legitimate sea captain for Great Britain. By 1690 he was a shipowner in New York City and obtained a commission to fight pirates in the Red Sea and the Indian Ocean. Having failed to receive payment for his commission, Kidd decided to turn to piracy himself at one point. He reportedly took an Armenian ship in payment for his services, an act for which he was declared a pirate. He returned to New York to argue his innocence, but was found guilty in an English court and sentenced to death. After the sentence had been carried out, however, some of his contemporaries would later question his guilt.

A widowed stepmother obtained a reading for her unmanageable sixteen-year-old stepson who had run away. In addition to a past life as the pirate, Captain Kidd, it was later discovered that the boy had also been the Irish adventurer and pickpocket, George Barrington.

(See also "Barrington, George.") The woman was told that the boy would not return to the United States until he was middle-aged:

> In entering this plane we find the entity comes under the influence of Neptune and Uranus, with those influences in Jupiter and in Mars. Hence the conditions as are exhibited in the present earth's plane in that of the love of the sea (see the body has gone to sea) . . .
>
> One that loves the use of firearms, and likes the display of same.
>
> One that in the present year finds the greatest changes coming in the life.
>
> One that will find many lands and many experiences in many lands, returning only to the present surroundings of birth in the middle of the life . . .
>
> One that will bring much joy and much sorrow to many, especially to the weaker sex, as termed . . .
>
> In the one before this we find in that of that entity often referred to as Captain Kidd, and the entity then gained in the first portion of the life, and in the latter portion gave much to others, though the experience to self rather severe. In the urge is found the love of the sea, of mystery, of those things as pertain to the mysterious, or of that ability to gain or place mystery in the eyes of others.   2213-1

In a previous life, [2213] had been in the English navy, also contributing to his love of the sea, adventure, and mystery. Earlier, he had been second in command of a Bedouin tribe, from which he had gained a love of the outdoors and the mysteries of nature. In Egypt he had also served those in power and had proved effective as a counselor to the ruler.

No follow-up reports are on file.

Kosciuszko, Tadeusz
1746-1817
Case 2327

A Polish army officer and statesman, Tadeusz Kosciuszko gained fame for his role in the U.S. War of Independence. Reportedly, he had journeyed to the Colonies because of his interest in their independence as well as because of a failed relationship. He fought on the side of the Colonists before returning to Poland in order to fight Russian invaders who occupied his homeland. After a term in a St. Petersburg prison, he traveled to both the United States and France attempting to promote Poland's independence. A brilliant strategist, he wrote *Manual on the Maneuvers of Horse Artillery*, which was used for years by the U.S. Army.

Because of her interest in Cayce's work, the mother of a thirty-seven-year-old advertising salesman (who had been born in St. Petersburg, Russia) obtained a reading for her son. Cayce stated that [2327] had abilities as a leader or a director, and that he would be a good companion. He was advised to get married as soon as he was able, for too often he had been a "wanderer." His talents would be best expressed in building his own home life:

> One that is a good friend, and a *bad* enemy. Hence cultivate friendships; even with those whom ye may find displeasing at the first encounter . . .
>
> Before this, then, the entity was in the land of the present sojourn. The entity came as an aid to those who were seeking self-government, then in the name Stephanus Cosiasco [Tadeusz Kosciuszko?]; hence a leader, a director, and one employed for making missions that dealt with conditions of authority—and the entity gained throughout.
>
> In the present there are the abilities as an executive, as a director; but the needs for the cultivating

of humor and wit, and not the great severity of the
soldier. Rather be the soldier in the *business* directions.   2327-1

He had also been in Greece, serving in the capacity of
what might be called a career counselor. From that experience, he could be extremely helpful in assisting individuals at discovering how they could be most helpful
to a business or corporation. He had also been a political advisor in ancient Egypt. No follow-up reports are on
file.

Lafitte, Jean
ca. 1780-ca. 1826
Case 2615

Jean Lafitte was a pirate who settled near the Baratarian
coast south of New Orleans and preyed on Spanish ships
in the Gulf of Mexico. In 1812, the British attempted to
buy Lafitte's assistance in attacking New Orleans. Lafitte
sent the British information to American authorities and
offered to aid the Americans if the U.S. pardoned him
and his men. Badly in need of men, General Andrew
Jackson accepted the offer, and President Madison pardoned Lafitte. Later, Lafitte and his men would return to
pirating on an island (Galveston) off the coast of Texas.

In 1941, a middle-aged male secretary was told that
he was an extremist and could channel his energies into
either very good or very bad directions. Possessing high
mental abilities and an innate desire to be of service to
others, he was told that his past incarnations were extremely varied. At one time, [2615] had been Jean Lafitte:

Then the entity was in that portion of the land
known as Louisiana—in the name Jean Lafitte.
There was much of accomplishment in material

ways, but because of the environs there was not accomplished the carrying through of that as desired
by the entity. This was because of associations with
others that were of a different intent or purpose.

Yet it may be said that the entity gained throughout the experience. And the determination to learn
more, to seek out sources of information—material
and spiritual—are the latent purposes of the entity
from that experience.   2615-1

According to Cayce, apparently Lafitte had an innate
love of the relationship between humanity and the soil.
That ability remained to this day. The reading also stated
that in spite of the pirate's reputation, much of Lafitte's
efforts had been with the intent of being of service to
others. Now, as then, [2615] sought personal understanding for his activities. Still considered unorthodox
in many of the things he would undertake, he was encouraged to direct his energies back toward the relationship of people and the soil. Past lives included innate
abilities with commerce, the disposition to work with
many different kinds of people, and one life (in Atlantis)
when he had satisfied his own physical appetites at the
expense of spiritual pursuits.

During the course of the reading, [2615] agreed with
many of the things that were said about him and believed that the information would mean a great deal to
him. However, no follow-up reports are on file.

Liszt, Franz
1811-1886
Case 2584

Born in Hungary, Franz Liszt was an innovative composer of Romantic music and the most celebrated pianist of the nineteenth century. Even as a child he showed

an aptitude for music. He began studying the piano when he was five and composing when he was eight. He debuted in Paris at the age of thirteen and began a career as a virtuoso all over Europe. By his thirties, he devoted himself to conducting and composing. He is best known for his symphonic poems, his piano compositions, and his religious music. After a failed marriage, he took minor holy orders from the Roman Catholic Church.

In a life reading given to an eleven-month-old boy, Cayce began by suggesting that the family call the child "Franz" as a nickname, since that was what the child would begin to call himself as soon as he could speak. The reading advised training and direction which would best enable the soul to express its innate talents:

> In the musical abilities should the entity be trained from the beginning. There is the natural intent and interest towards things of the artistic nature and temperament. There are the abilities to use the voice, as well as the abilities in playing most *any* instrument—if the opportunity is given; especially in the composition, in the natures of composition as well as the playing itself. Symphonies, all forms of musical interludes and the like, should be the trainings to which the entity would be subjected— that it may be given the greater opportunities. And, as soon as he is capable of such, insist upon beginning with the piano—as a playing, as a means of entertaining. And the natural ear for harmony will soon be indicated in the activities of the entity . . .
>
> Before this the entity was in the Austrian or Hungarian land. There the entity was an unusual individual, in the name Liszt; being a composer as well as a musician. And as its activities through the experience were such as to make for certain characters of music, these in part will be of special interest

to the entity in the present. The comparison may be easily seen, to be sure, as to the faults, the failures, as well as the activities in which the entity then throughout the experience rose to its place or position in the musical world.

That is why, then, the nickname Franz is suggested; for the entity was Franz Liszt.   2584-1

In the past, [2584] had been among the chief musicians for both David and Solomon, and had been responsible for music in the Temple. From that experience he had gained a love of religious music that "appealed to the minds of those who would come to worship." In ancient Egypt, he had been one who created chants that facilitated physical healing in the temples. From these past experiences he possessed the ability to create music that appealed to every aspect of an individual: physically, emotionally, and spiritually. Cayce suggested that if the child were given the proper training he would play an important role in American music.

After the reading, the child's grandmother expressed her thrill at being able "to have the opportunity to give this child his musical education." She noted that "we all love music in our family and the baby already hears symphonies. His father has a fine collection of records of the best symphonic music and is *quite* musical himself."

A year later it was noted, "[2584] has already started with music. He is charming and a beautiful little boy." No additional follow-up reports are on file.

Louis XV
1710-1774
Case 1001

Louis XV is best known for his mostly ineffectual rule, his quest for sensual pleasures, and his liaisons with various mistresses. He succeeded the throne at the age of five and was guided by chief ministers who governed the country cautiously and economically. During that time he was called "well-beloved" by his people; years later, however, he would narrowly escape an assassination attempt. At the age of thirty-three, Louis chose to rule without the aid of a chief minister. After that time, his reign would be marked by a series of disastrous wars, the loss of foreign territories, financial difficulties, infighting among his lesser ministers, and conflicts with the nobles, all contributing to the French Revolution fifteen years after his death.

In 1930, a twenty-three-year-old man obtained a reading about his past lives. Involved in real estate, he also had a great love for music. Already, he had been a patient in the Cayce Hospital, where he had received a number of readings about his epileptic seizures. During the course of the reading, Cayce suggested that [1001] needed to find himself, and that his health challenge was simply a condition which could enable him to be less inclined to pursue sensuality and more inclined to be "helpful, mindful, considerate, [and] understanding" of others. By so doing, he could bring much to many and help himself in the process:

> . . . for in the one as before this may there be said in the present, how has the mighty fallen—yet that as is innate, that even in feature of expression, that innately held, may be seen and met in the present; for in the one before this we find as Louis 15th the entity reigned in France, and in a mighty manner— being of those that sought for the gratification of many of selfish desires, gaining and losing. Gaining in the service as *given to* many, in the consideration as was given to many. Losing in the aggrandizing of selfish interests in self, in bodily desire, in the in-

temperance of those elements of mind *and* body—
these brought destructive forces in the experience
of the entity ...   1001-7

During a lifetime in the Holy Land, he had been involved with the establishment of music in the temples.
In Egypt he had created codes of moral conduct, which
had been completely rebelled against during his lifetime
in France. He was encouraged to find balance in body,
mind, and spirit, and to discover the reasonableness of
moral application in his present experience. Only as he
pursued music and poetry, and how they could glorify
the spirit within individuals, "will the entity succeed, will
the entity develop, will the gains be the greater." It was
the pursuit of music and not sensuality that could help
him help himself and others.

Years later, it was noted that the young man never
seemed to grasp the rationale behind his being encouraged to pursue a less sensual lifetime. "At times he would
go away for days at a time, on drinking sprees and riot-
ous night-life excursions. His mother would finally lo-
cate him in some hotel, foot the bills, and bring him
home." No additional reports are on file.

Louis XVI
1754-1793
Case 5618

Louis XVI is best known for having been the last
French monarch as well as for his marriage to Marie
Antoinette. He succeeded to the throne after his grandfather's (Louis XV's) reign of mismanagement and failed
in a series of halfhearted reform efforts. French partici-
pation in the American Revolution on the side of the
Colonists against the British increased government debt
and created demands for liberty at home. Meanwhile,

Louis was absorbed in family life, hunting, and mechanical arts, for he was a skilled locksmith. He was overthrown in 1789 and held prisoner until his execution by guillotine in 1793 for allegedly conspiring against the Revolutionary government.

A fifty-nine-year-old doctor of osteopathy and enthusiast of the Edgar Cayce work was told that he was a very caring soul, always putting others before himself and always seeking to be of service to those around him. The reading stated that he had been Louis XVI:

> In the one before this we find the entity then in power, in the rule as in that known as France, and in that as of the entity then known as Louis 16th, and the entity gained through the oppression to the entity and those about same, losing in that of the ability to apply *own* will with reference to good of others. Hence we see the two combating influences in the present as an urge. One that loves those of the intrinsic conditions as respecting detail in any mechanical devices, and the entity would have made a wonderful clock repairer, or clocksmith. The entity finds also that urge as pertains to those of medicine, and of mechano-therapy, as was first given then by this entity during the sojourn in the earth's plane.   5618-8

According to the reading, [5618] was married to the same woman who had been Marie Antoinette and their present son had also been their son in France. (See also "Marie Antoinette.") As a result, the three were very closely attached to one another. Dr. [5618] was told that he had also been Romulus, one of the legendary founders of Rome. (See also "Romulus.") In Persia he had assisted those who were suffering in body and in mind, which had given rise to his desire to become a doctor in the present. In Babylon he had been a builder and possessed innate talents as a sculptor. From a lifetime in ancient Egypt, he had gained skills as a counselor and had talents to bring harmony among peoples. Throughout all of his incarnations, one of his primary desires was to be of service to others.

Dr. [5618]'s desire to be of service led him and his family to move to Virginia Beach in the spring of 1928. There, he set up practice and became the house physician for the Cayce Hospital when it opened in the fall of 1928. Unfortunately, he died in the fall of 1929.

Mann, Horace
1796-1859
Case 1859

Horace Mann is considered the father of American public education. Raised in poverty, he managed to attend Brown University, chose the law as his career, and eventually served in the Massachusetts House of Representatives and the state Senate. During eleven years with the state board of education, he strove for the establishment of universal education in nonsectarian schools supported by taxes and taught by qualified professional teachers. In 1848 he became a member of the U.S. Congress and in 1853 he was made president of Antioch College, where he served until his death.

In 1939, a twenty-six-year-old writer, actor, and teacher, who professed a love of poetry, was told that only a few of his previous incarnations were being given because "these in the next seven years will be the leading influences." In his life just previous to the present, he had been born during a period of turmoil that followed the American Revolution:

Hence we find it was a period of unrest, yet in the

latter portion of that experience, in those periods
when the entity acted as the teacher, in the name
Horace Mann, the entity brought the establishing
of the principles and factors that became and are as
an influence in the lives of the many—as to principles and tenets and experiences.

As to the application of same in the present—the
dislike, as indicated, of giving or receiving criticism;
but abilities to choose to work out from *lowly* experiences that which is ideal in material as well as in
spiritual things—*if self* and the aggrandizing of self
is left out!   1859-1

In Greece he had been one who had turned the politics and events of the day into stage presentations and
plays. For much of that life he had let spiritual pursuits
fall behind his desire for material rewards and praise.
Innately, he possessed talents as a writer, an actor, or a
commentator upon daily life. In his present life, [1859]
said that he had a strong attraction to Jesus. According
to his reading, during the time of Jesus, [1859] had been
a herdsman and a skilled musician, and had witnessed
the angels sing above the hills of Bethlehem. In Atlantis,
he had been part of the migration to other lands during
the destruction of the continent.

The reading told him that he had a tendency toward
self-sufficiency which he needed to overcome. He was
advised to pursue his abilities with music and acting focused in such a manner as to help individuals recall their
relationship to the Creative Forces. If he used his talents
in this direction, he was promised they would be "multi-
plied some thirty, some sixty, some an hundredfold."

No follow-up reports are on file.

Marat, Jean Paul
1743-1793
Case 960

Jean Paul Marat is considered one of the most notorious figures of the French Revolution. A physician and French journalist, Marat rose to fame as the editor of the radical newspaper *L'Ami du Peuple* ("The Friend of the People"), in which he denounced French ministers, deputies, and even the king. He called for the creation of a new government and the execution of those who opposed the French Revolution. In spite of his intense opposition to many individuals, Marat was immensely popular with the common people for he possessed compassion for the poor and a deep concern for social injustice. He was later assassinated by his rivals.

A thirteen-year-old deaf boy, known as a "problem child," had received a series of readings for his deafness. Finally, a life reading was obtained in 1927. As far as previous lifetimes, "In the one before this, we find in that period when the Revolution in France brought the uprising of the common people . . . in the name then—Marat." (960-4) Apparently, [960] still had trouble understanding why his own ego should be subjugated or directed by others. In spite of his temperament, the parents were told that the boy could bring "much joy, much happiness" to others.

Cayce stated that the boy possessed deep feelings of love for others and didn't ever want to see anyone suffer. The child also often found himself easily misunderstood. He had a strong conviction for "*right for right's sake*" and would make a good lawyer. During previous incarnations, he had experienced persecution in Jerusalem as a result of his spiritual beliefs. As a ruler in Peru, he had misused and abused his own power. Cayce stated that the boy's future depended upon where his abilities were directed, and the parents were advised that the creation of "all good must be founded upon the relation of an entity to its Giver."

Because of a series of physical readings, by 1931 the boy's hearing had improved although not cured. According to the file notation in October of that year, "He was home for the weekend; attending college and getting along beautifully. The parents were very grateful for the help which had been given to them and their son through the readings."

Nearly forty years later, in August of 1969, [960] contacted A.R.E. and indicated that he was employed as a divisional manager for a large brokerage firm. He requested copies of his readings and stated, "There may be some pertinent observations from my experiences of the past forty years which I would like to pass on to you after studying them." In October of that same year, he stated that he was still studying the information. Unfortunately, Mr. [960] never followed up with a supplemental report.

Marie Antoinette
1755-1793
Case 760

Marie Antoinette was queen while her husband, Louis XVI, was king of France. Unpopular among the French, she was considered extravagant in her spending, prone to extramarital affairs, and generous with a few court favorites. In spite of the growing pressure for a reformed monarchy, Marie Antoinette opposed the reforms proposed by the king's ministers. With the exception of a small circle of friends, she withdrew from French society, an action which only increased her unpopularity. She was accused unjustly of having an immoral affair with a Roman Catholic cardinal, which led to a further discredit of the monarchy. The daughter of Maria Theresa of Austria, she was seen as an untrustworthy foreigner and was eventually accused of aiding Austria in a planned invasion of France. Popular hatred of the queen contributed to the overthrow of the monarchy and her eventual death by guillotine.

The wife of a doctor was told that she had acquired two very different inclinations in regard to her reactions toward other people because of her deeds from the past. Over a period of time, she had received a series of readings for her problems with lumbago, sciatica, nervousness and anxiety, and poor eliminations. Described as "regal bearing—sort of a queen of a big family . . . [and] the last word on any decision of importance," she was told that her present husband had been Louis XVI of France when she had been Marie Antoinette. (See also "Louis XVI.")

> As to appearances, these we find have much to do with the various and varied conditions as are manifest and exhibited in the present life.
> In the one, then, before this, we find in that of the Queen who was beheaded, in that of Marie Theresa, or Marie Antoinette, as known in the historic forces, and in that we find both development and the retarding, for the beginning of the force as exercised in that plane brought much good and much bad to many people, and all must be met in the earth's plane . . .   760-4

From lifetimes in Egypt and Greece, [760] had acquired the desire and the ability to help those she loved, especially men, in their careers and their work. In Greece, in addition to acquiring talents at creating a home and raising a family, she had been a skilled seamstress. In Egypt, while she had focused on assisting those in her life, she had also labored to preserve historic relics. From that same Egyptian life, she possessed abilities in art, especially in decoration.

Mrs. [760] was told that her inclination to assist the men in her life had become a negative influence in her French incarnation when she had attempted to control her husband, providing him with poor advice, especially in regard to his relationship to the common people. The tendency to think herself better than the average individual had originated during a lifetime in Peru. At that time, she had sought to control others by constantly reminding them of the realities of life and their own foolishness at possessing any higher hopes, dreams, or aspirations in the face of such realism. If the urges of the Peruvian lifetime combined with the temper of her incarnation as Marie Antoinette, it could be a truly destructive influence in the present.

Cayce stated that the greatest abilities she had in the present were talents in creating a home, as well as the ability to bring people together for a common goal. She was told that she would make a wonderful nurse and could find much satisfaction in assisting others.

For a time, Mrs. [760] was being considered for the position of house matron while the Cayce Hospital was under construction. With that in mind, she provided many suggestions in terms of the building's design, layout, and amenities. When the hospital was opened, her husband became physician in charge, until his death a year later. While he lived, she was truly his help-meet.

One of the only reports on file is from 1955, when a notation was made of the fact that Mrs. [760] seemed to be a collector of silver, linens, furniture, art, etc. According to Gladys Davis, "When she died, she left trunks of elaborately embroidered linens. All her life, since a very young girl, she never sat down even for a few minutes without picking up her embroidery. When traveling by train [she] would never go from one car to another; couldn't stand the rumbling noise, etc." Gladys asked the question, "Could this be a throw-back to the ride to her death over cobblestones . . . ?"

Marshall, John
1755-1835
Case 5352

John Marshall is considered the principal founder of U.S. constitutional law. The fourth chief justice of the Supreme Court, he helped to establish judicial review over acts of the other branches of the U.S. government. He served in the Continental Army under Washington and eventually wrote a five-volume work about the first president.

In 1944, the grandmother of young boy, nearly three years old, was told that the family had been given "the responsibility of an unusual entity" and that he should be "trained in all manners for a jurist." (5352-1) The only incarnation provided in the reading was one as John Marshall.

The family was advised to be extremely careful during the child's formative years. They were never to lie to the child or to force him to do something through half-truths. It was suggested that they read a biography of John Marshall and realize that the same tendencies would be part of their child's present experience. They were encouraged to train the boy in gentleness, kindness, and positive reinforcement. Additionally, they were told to be wary of problems with health and temperature extremes, and were encouraged to seek further guidance for the child when he was ten.

No follow-up reports are on file.

Martin, Saint
ca. 316-397
Case 3202

The son of a pagan soldier, Saint Martin of Tours originally joined the Roman army but converted to Christianity and became convinced that a Christian ought not to
bear arms against other Christians. When charged with
cowardice for his refusal to fight, he offered to stand in
front of the Roman battle line armed with only a cross.
He opposed the killing of heretics and gained a reputation as a miracle worker. Considered one of the fathers
of Western monasticism, he founded the first monastery
in Gaul. One of the legends associated with Martin is his
cutting his coat in half to clothe a poor beggar in the
freezing cold of winter.

Parents of a seven-year-old boy were told that their
child's life could develop along the lines of two contra-
dictory experiences. His training and upbringing would
determine the direction his life unfolded. Apparently,
the boy possessed an innate inclination toward laziness
and unless overcome, he would become indolent and
idle in the present, "For, the entity before this was a patron saint of France, and yet so lazy as to be expressed in
the present." (3202-1)

Although not normally encouraged, Cayce told the
parents to interest the boy in his own past lives, which
would be stimulating to him. If this were done, by the
age of fifty-four, he would have the opportunity to assist
in the spiritual welfare of many individuals. Cayce stated
that the boy possessed an innate ability with languages
and should be trained in French, Latin, and Spanish. His
talents could be directed in diplomatic activities and in
the facilitating of relationships among countries.

In previous lives he had been in the Holy Land and
had been familiar with the teachings of the apostle Pe-

ter. In ancient Egypt, he had been a diplomat in charge of relationships with other lands. The boy's parents were encouraged to make the *principles* of Christianity a part of their child's upbringing and to make certain he found interests to help him overcome his laziness.

No follow-up reports are on file.

Molière
1622-1673
Case 2814

Molière was the stage name of Jean Baptiste Poquelin. A French dramatist and theater manager, he became known as one of the greatest of French writers, directors, and actors for his genius with comedy. Raised the son of a furniture merchant and upholsterer, he was a master of sophisticated comedy and developed a number of classical caricatures (such as "the religious hypocrite," "the dupe," "the social climber," etc.) which endeared him to French bourgeois audiences.

In 1942, Edgar Cayce began a life reading for an eight-month-old boy by stating, "Quite an interesting figure, as the entity has been through the experiences in the earth!" As was always the case for children, the reading reminded the parents of their important role in the raising of their son. The boy's innate interests were varied. He would be talented in music and drama. Cayce stated that the boy would express himself through philosophy, psychology, and the dramatic arts. He would also have abilities in décor and furnishings, "For, in the appearance before this, the entity entered as Jean Poquelin, known as Molière the great French dramatist."

For, as Molière he also attained to the associations with Louis 13th in arranging his own chambers, his own various places of dwelling and such;

and these as combined with the argumentations, the philosophies. For, he will have many peculiar ones as to why he does this or that, but you may never fear but what he will always give—even in his younger years—the reason why he did this or that! He will never answer "I don't know." He will always answer with the cause, this or that, philosophizing. And thus, in the early preparations, the training should be towards psychology and such subjects that deal with the mind—even in the early period. Take the time to explain this, that and the other; and he will ask more than the usual questions asked by the young!   2814-1

No additional past-life information was provided.

In 1942, his grandmother noted: "[2814] lifts his brows in a most fetching way—quite unusual! Molière made a big hit on the stage the way he lifted his brows."

One of the few reports on file states that [2814] served in World War II and returned home unharmed.

Mullens, Priscilla
ca. 1625
Case 1318

Best known from Henry Wadsworth Longfellow's *The Courtship of Miles Standish*, Priscilla Mullens was asked if she would be willing to marry Miles Standish (ca. 1584-1656) by his friend, John Alden (1599-1687). As the story goes, Mullens ended up marrying Alden instead. John Alden had been the first Pilgrim to set foot on Plymouth Rock, and the marriage between the two occurred within three years of the *Mayflower's* arrival in Massachusetts.

A middle-aged woman who had become a spiritual teacher in the Orient received a life reading in 1937. She was told:

Before this we find the expression or activity of the entity in the earlier portion of the American experience has brought, does bring to the entity its activities in this experience in the present; in and about what is now known as Salem and Provincetown, during those early portions of that activity when the entity—then Priscilla—made for that which has become as a poem, given to the peoples of the experience as in love, faith, hope; though questioned by those that were of that intent to impel by man-made laws the activities of individuals, of group associations.

Hence we find in the experience of the entity in the present those abilities for the analyzing of associations with individuals, whether in the home or whether in their relationships in the material activities, are a part of the entity's *mental* abilities.

1318-1

Additionally, she was told that in Rome she had been a counselor to those in authority and in Egypt she had been a priestess in one of the temples. Cayce told her that her abilities in the present had to do with the field of metaphysics and helping human beings understand their relationship to one another.

No reports are on file.

Nero
37-68
Case 33

Nero was the last Roman emperor of the line of Julius Caesar. He is remembered for his unstable character, his court's extravagances, and his cruelty. Known for the executions of those who got in his way, he put his own mother and his wife to death. He began the first major

Roman persecution of the Christians. His reign caused public unrest and made enemies throughout the empire. In 64, a great fire ruined Rome and Nero rebuilt the city; however, rumors persisted that Nero himself had set the fire to make room for his new palace. Finally, the Roman senate condemned him to death, and he reportedly fled and committed suicide.

In 1926, a twenty-four-year-old man contacted Edgar Cayce for a physical reading. He was an ex-coal miner who had been paralyzed from the neck down four years previously in a car wreck. Cayce began the physical reading by stating that a life reading would be much more interesting. The reading advised an operation performed at "Johns Hopkins, Mayo's, General Hospital, New York, or . . . the Institute in Pittsburgh." Detailed instructions for the operation were given which recommended that portions of the spinal column be removed and rewired. Although not a cure and [33] would be stooped, Cayce said that he would have some degree of locomotion.

At the end of the reading, [33] was told, "for . . . many of these conditions are merited through those actions of the mental forces and the spiritual forces of the body . . . " (33-1) And then under his breath Cayce added, "Hence that as given in the first. See, this is Nero." The young man was not told of his connection to Nero, but Mr. Cayce did try to convince him to get the operation that had been recommended.

One of the few reports on file states, "A form letter sent from our office in 1940 came back marked 'deceased.' For eighteen years he was completely helpless and thus entirely dependent upon charitable Christians for every detail of his care."

Neuendorff, Adolph
1843-1897
Case 5398

Neuendorff was born in Hamburg and taken to America at the age of twelve. He is known as a pianist, concert violinist, and a prominent conductor and composer of symphonies, overtures, cantatas, and comic operas. Before his death, he was the conductor of the Metropolitan Opera House in New York.

In one of the last readings given before he became ill, Edgar Cayce told the parents of a ten-week-old boy that—with the proper upbringing—their child's talent lay in a musical direction:

> . . . one gifted, as will be indicated in the unfolding of the abilities of the body in that called the higher arts, especially of the use of the voice—all of its abilities as a composer, as a singer, should be those things to which those responsible in the present should direct this entity, for this entity was among those who first began to attempt to make music, especially American music, and yet the name, to many, unless there is the study of same would indicate other things. For the name in the experience before this was Neuendorff—but study what that means, and what he did . . . not merely for meeting the problems of the character of voice, of music, but give the entity the advantage, especially, of piano and stringed instruments of every nature, but the voice will be noteworthy, and such as to make a great contribution to true American music, if there are those directions as indicated, and yet, as has been indicated . . . attempt that of not answering, or attempting to deceive, ye may make a singer on the street, and not a good one, at that!   5398-1

As long as the parents gave the boy the upbringing he needed, he would succeed.

Cayce said that innately the boy possessed a great deal of imagination and was quite sensitive. During the time of Jesus, he had been present as a child at the miracle of the feeding of the five thousand. Cayce stated, "Hence, you will always find the entity ready to eat when it is time to eat, and he will expect it to be there, no matter where it comes from!" Later in that life, [5398] had become an inspirational singer of psalms, journeying and assisting Paul (and others) in their travels to the various churches. He had also been a psalmist during an earlier experience in the Holy Land. In ancient Egypt, he had been trained as a teacher and a lecturer and had become an emissary to other lands. During an incarnation in Atlantis, [5398] had been a royal prince.

The boy's parents were advised to teach their child by example and to guide him in a musical direction. Four years later, the boy's mother reported: "[5398] has all the tendencies of a musical career . . . " In 1956, [5398]'s mother added:

> He has composed about five selections, one of which I feel is very good. He doesn't do so well in school, probably because he daydreams so much. His teacher told me there are times when he will look right at her and she knows he isn't hearing a word she is saying, that he is somewhere away off. One day he was working on his arithmetic and stopped in the middle of it. I asked him, "Aren't you going to finish your lesson before you stop?" He answered that he was hearing music and wanted to go right to the piano and see if he could play it. His difficulty is mostly, so far, in writing it down. He wants to get a harp—doesn't like violin music—had an accordion at one time but does most of his prac-

ticing on the piano. He says that "sometimes music comes to my mind and I have to stop whatever I am doing and go to the piano and play."

One of the last reports on file was written during the boy's twentieth year by an aunt:

[5398] is now in his second year of a music college, majoring in music. He is a very fine boy, tall and handsome, quiet and home loving. All through high school he had his own band. One summer they played professionally; he was manager of the band . . . [5398] played the organ; he had the record of being the only "standing up" organ player in the business . . . This past summer he has been working with his father, [1710], in the construction business, to earn money to help with his college expenses. He definitely shows all the signs of preparing himself for a musical career. He has a splendid speaking and singing voice, and, of course, was always the spokesman for his band.

Oglethorpe, James
1696-1785
Case 4915

A British general and philanthropist, James Edward Oglethorpe founded the colony of Georgia and served as its first governor. A member of Parliament, Oglethorpe secured a charter to colonize Georgia in 1733, the year he settled Savannah. Originally, he saw the colony as a place where the poor and destitute could began again and where persecuted Protestant sects could worship freely. Oglethorpe returned to England in 1743, where he resumed his career in Parliament.

Although he never received a personal reading himself, a forty-two-year-old musician and dramatist was given case number [4915] to preserve his identity. A number of other individuals received readings and were told that they had been related to James Oglethorpe in their most recent lifetimes and that Oglethorpe was now reincarnated as Mr. [4915].

Paine, Thomas
1737-1809
Case 3031

Thomas Paine was born in England but emigrated to America in 1774 at the recommendation of Benjamin Franklin. He received immediate recognition for the publication of his *Common Sense* pamphlet, which sold 100,000 copies in three months and provided a persuasive argument for colonial independence. Long sympathetic to the poor and unfortunate, he later called for the elimination of poverty, illiteracy, war, and unemployment. After the war, Paine moved to England, where he was charged with treason, so he fled to France and remained there for fifteen years. He became unpopular in the U.S. because of his criticism of George Washington. When he returned to the states in 1802, he found his contribution toward independence largely forgotten and died in virtual poverty.

A forty-year-old teacher and training specialist for the War Department was told that "in common parlance—he will either excel or make a mess of many things!" According to his reading, he had often been in the earth when new beginnings were in the offing. From a lifetime in Atlantis, he had an innate tendency toward extremes and needed to find balance and a continuity of purpose, physically, mentally, and spiritually. Although he possessed high mental abilities, he could fall again into his tendency toward extremes—or he could become a writer.

Before this, then, we find that the entity was in the earth during that period following that called the American Revolution . . .

Through that particular period the entity was not only questioned as to his mode of reason but as to the manner of application. Yet we find the lack of the entity's awareness through that experience, or in the choice of self, of being classed in that category of those disbelieving in the divinity of those forces manifested. And yet the entity must come to that awareness that each soul, each entity, is divine in its *own* right. And as it applies the more of the universal consciousness it may become as the savior, as the prophet, as one consciously aware of being at one with that Creative Force.

Then the entity was known as Tom Paine. In the experience the entity contributed much to the factors having to do with man's individual thought, as to man's rights in speech as well as in the form of worship.   3031-1

In Rome, he had a minor part in the persecution of the Christians. During that time he had essentially noted and correlated the activities of the group, detailing its political, moral, and religious doctrines. In Egypt, he had been part of a group that defied the ability of the ruler to have any authority over other individuals. In Atlantis, he had forsaken some of his spiritual principles for the acquisition of knowledge. In the present, he was encouraged to pursue spirituality and to discover his own spiritual beliefs. At the same time, he was encouraged to let writing be his greatest outlet.

As it turns out, [3031] had been working on several writing pieces at the time of his reading, including a "mathematical psychology book" and a movie script. In 1957, he requested a copy of his life reading and appar-

ently continued to be a part of A.R.E. activities throughout the 1960s. It was reported in 1968 that he had died;
however, no detailed reports about how his life (or his
writing) unfolded are on file.

Pocahontas
ca. 1595-1617
Case 324

Although disputed by some historians, legend has it
that Pocahontas, daughter of Chief Powhatan, threw
herself over the body of Captain John Smith when he was
about to be killed by her tribe. Afterward, Pocahontas
became the intermediary between her father and the
Colonists. Later, she reportedly had her father send food
to the starving Jamestown settlement. She became a
convert to Christianity and in 1614, with her father's ap-
proval, married a successful tobacco planter, John Rolfe.
The marriage created eight years of peace between the
Indians and the settlement. After her marriage, she became Lady Rebecca Rolfe and journeyed to London,
where she charmed society and the royal palace. Before
having the opportunity to return to the Colonies, however, she contracted smallpox and died.

The grandmother of a three-year-old girl was told, in
1934, that her granddaughter would be very self-certain
in her activities and that she would marry early. She
would possess talents in music and would forever be interested in "new associations, new relations, new activities in the experience of not only self but those about the
entity." During the course of the reading, Cayce stated
that the vibration of the color purple would have a very
positive influence upon the child, somehow affecting
the girl physically, mentally, and spiritually.

As to the experiences of the entity in the earth:

Before this (that influences the entity in the early portion of the development in this particular experience or environ) we find the entity was in the present land of nativity, adjoining those influences in which the entity came into this present activity. For the entity then was among those people that inhabited the land when there were the settlings of the English in the land; being then a daughter of the Chief of those people that made peace with those in and about Williamsburg, Jamestown, and the adjoining lands; and was a Princess then, in the name Ptheula . . . Its meaning was that it made for the closer relationships with those over whom and with whom the Chief ruled; or peace among the brethren.   324-5

Although [324]'s reading did not mention the name "Pocahontas," in a reading given to her grandfather (289-9), it was stated that [324] had been the daughter of Chief Powhatan and had been sent to England during that same incarnation. Gladys Davis inferred from this that [324] was, in fact, the Indian princess.

Other lives included an incarnation in France when she had been a royal attendant to the king. In Palestine, she had worked in the household of Herod Antipas and had become a member of the Christian sect after witnessing miraculous healings. In Persia, she had been one who had initiated the call to worship through music—a practice, the readings stated, that was still being observed by Muslims and East Indians. In Egypt, she had taken part in temple services and had been involved in dance and the music of the harp, and helping individuals find their connection to the Creative Forces. From several lifetimes, she had acquired the innate love of physical activities and the great outdoors.

The grandmother was told that the child's early life

would involve establishing a home, but later she would turn to music and entertainment or those things which pertained to the outdoors. Cayce told those who were responsible for the child, "Then, as has been given, train the child in the way it should go; when it is old it will not depart from same."

The first report on file is from 1934 and states that [324] was extremely cross and agitated with another child who was her playmate. Nothing the playmate did seemed to please [324]. Finally, in order to experiment with what the Cayce reading had said about color, the child's grandmother hung a purple dress from the chandelier with the excuse that she was airing it out. Almost immediately, [324] stopped being irritable and neither the playmate nor the grandmother had any trouble with the girl for the rest of the day.

When she was five, [324]'s schoolteacher made note of the child's gift for dancing and entertainment. At the age of seventeen, [324] married a plumber apprentice. The two had a baby girl the following year. No additional follow-up reports are on file.

Pompadour, Madame de
1721-1764
Case 1849

Madame de Pompadour was an influential mistress of Louis XV and a notable patron of the arts and literature. (See also "Louis XV.") She was educated to be the wife of a rich man, which came to pass when she married a financier. Afterward, she became known as one of the shining stars of French society. She separated from her husband when she became the king's official mistress in 1745. Naturally artistic and musical, she was responsible for the king's entertainment and helped to design building projects, including the Place de la Concorde and the

Petit Trianon Palace at Versailles.

A thirty-seven-year-old woman obtained a life reading in July of 1939. A single businesswoman and the owner of a personal therapy salon, she had been working on perfecting a "reducing cream" which she hoped to market. She was told that the fleur-de-lis had an innate effect upon her and she was encouraged to use it in some fashion. Possessing many talents, she was told that her abilities should be directed toward helping others or else her talents would mean nothing. Apparently, her life could take on very different directions depending on how she chose to help others.

Before this we find the entity (among those having the greater present influence) was in the French land in the periods when Louis was the King.

Hence, as has been indicated, the purposes, the signs, the symbols, the heraldry of that land are of particular interest, are of particular import in the very nature of the entity . . .

For the abilities of the entity in that sojourn were used in making relationships with and comparisons of those in the Court throughout that experience; being very active in the *power* the entity wielded over those peoples as well as the ruler himself. Hence these made for advancements and for retardments; for confusions, for likes and dislikes.

The entity was named then Pompeia (?). In the experience the entity found itself with such abilities that in the present these are seen in the abilities for the carriage, the dress, the abilities to attract, the abilities to confuse, the abilities to keep many guessing, the abilities to go to the extreme—these all arise from the activities of the entity through that sojourn. 1849-2

During a lifetime in Rome when she had become interested in the activities of the Christian sect, she had again been a close associate of the individual "in authority, in power." In ancient Egypt, she was a close companion of the High Priest and had aided individuals during their personal purification in the temple services. From that Egyptian lifetime, she possessed a talent for assisting individuals in beautifying themselves: "Hence the abilities to prepare lotions, powders, or to apply for bodily needs those things that would make for the better physical expression, become channels in which the entity may become more and more an adept in being a constructive influence in the lives and the experiences of others." Finally, in Atlantis, she had counseled those who were leaving the continent during the second destruction.

She was told that if she wanted to be a material success, she had to become a spiritual success in terns of her purposes and her desires. [1849] would find the greatest happiness by helping others.

A sister submitted a report in 1961: "[1849] was in D.C. for several years; she practiced physiotherapy under a N.Y. license; she married a Canadian subject; he died while they were living in Cuba." After her husband's death, she lived in the West Indies, where she worked with the natives, showing them how to take care of themselves. While there, the natives called her "Little White Mother." According to her sister, she died a few years later.

Putnam, Israel
1718-1790
Case 2533

Born in Salem (now Danvers), Massachusetts, Israel Putnam was an American soldier who left his farm to serve in the French and Indian War, where he attained the rank of lieutenant colonel. Shipwrecked in 1762 in a skirmish against Havana, he was one of the few individuals on board to survive. He had numerous military adventures, giving him the name "Old Put" and causing him to be something of a folk hero. His military experience led the Continental Congress to appoint him a general during the American Revolution. However, he never measured up to the high hopes that George Washington had for him and, in 1777, he was reprimanded for insubordination. Historians generally agree that his rank and later assignments exceeded his talents.

In 1941, while giving a reading to a thirty-six-year-old insurance agent, Cayce stated that it was apparent from some of the information he was seeing in the akashic records that there was a variance between man-made records and true history. Apparently, Cayce saw a more talented soul in the individual of General Israel Putnam than had been previously recorded:

Not all of the appearances in the earth plane may be given at once, yet these are chosen as the indications to which the emotions and activities of the body turn—and that there may be the helpful forces:

Before this the entity was in the land of the present nativity, but in quite a different portion of the land; during those periods just before and during the American Revolution.

The entity was a character there, the story of whose power and influence wrought has not been completely given. For, the entity was first a philosopher; a teacher, a farmer, a general in the Continental army; the entity who left his plow, his oxen, and went in defense of an ideal, a purpose; one who defended itself by riding down . . . very steep steps to escape from those who would produce or bring about activities in the experience of the entity that would have been at variance to the purposes of the entity.

Through the experience the entity gained, not only in its purpose but in the material manifestations—in that it was more and more selfless, more and more purposeful for the greater good, not only materially but mentally and spiritually; that men might be free.

From that experience we find in the present the love of, and the search for, unusual historical facts; the love of certain characters of books of adventure, and of those pertaining to the basis upon which various thoughts or movements have been founded— whether religious, political or economic. These are the expressions found in the present experience of the entity.

The name then was Israel Putnam.   2533-1

In Rome he had been a political guide, analyzing individuals for their ability to serve individuals and groups in various capacities. At that time, he eventually became a part of the work of the early church in Laodicea. Earlier, as a keeper of the treasury under Croesus, [2533] had analyzed various portions of the Persian Empire for its ability to pay taxes. There, he had gained an innate love of precious stones. In ancient Egypt, he had acted in the capacity of what might be called "social services," insuring that children and families were provided for in the event of death or disability.

Mr. [2533] was advised, "The fields of activity and of service materially have to do with statistics, or of political natures, or of insurance. These will find the greater response in the entity." He was also encouraged to create and write instructions for others who wished to pursue the same type of work. He was reminded of the faith he had nurtured in both New England and Laodicea and was encouraged to make it a part of his present experience.

After the reading, Mr. [2533] commented: "So perfect, can see myself all the way through it. I'm glad it didn't tell me to change in my work. So many people go into the insurance business as a last resort, when they can't do anything else, but I *chose* insurance—I gave up another job to go into it. Have always been interested in precious stones—am wearing a sapphire that means a great deal to me . . . "

For his own information, [2533] made several trips to Danvers, Massachusetts, and often inquired about the life history of Israel Putnam.

A 1963 notation from Gladys Davis states: "To this date Mr. [2533] has remained an active, participating member of the A.R.E." In the 1960s, his connection with Israel Putnam was detailed in Ruth Montgomery's book, *Here and Hereafter.* Afterward, [2533] freely discussed his life reading with anyone who inquired. A number of letters were sent to Mr. [2533] in care of the Edgar Cayce Foundation, to which he was happy to respond.

In 1972, a letter was received by the Cayce Foundation and stated, "Since we own the farmhouse where Gen. Putnam died and much of the land that he was to have worked on and planted—would it be possible to have a copy of this reading?" The letter was given to [2533], still active in the Cayce work, who replied:

Obviously it was not by chance that I was in the library of the Association for Research and Enlightenment, Inc., doing some research for a lecture on a subject of interest to me, when your letter to the Edgar Cayce Library was delivered.

Mr. [2533] stated that he was planning to take a two-to-three-week trip to Connecticut and Massachusetts "to see if I pick up any memories of the Putnam incarnation." He offered to talk to the owners of the property when he was in the area. No reports of that meeting are on file.

The last entry is from 1987, when it was noted that Mr. [2533] had died at the age of 83.

Randolph, John
1773-1833
Case 5008

John Randolph was a Southern planter who became a brilliant U.S. political leader and statesman. He is best known for his opposition to a strong centralized government, favoring instead the individual rights of states. Once elected to the U.S. House of Representatives, within a couple of years he was made chairman of the House Ways and Means Committee. A brilliant and sarcastic debater, he often denounced those who challenged his opposition to national programs and federal legislation. In spite of his political talent, throughout his life he was often plagued by ill health.

In 1944, a ten-month-old boy was told "he should have one day a voice in the affairs of the state and of the nation."

For the entity in the early activities in this land, in the southern area, was John Randolph II. In the House of Delegates his activities were such that the peoples from other lands were the opponents in regard to the measures that were a part of the experience.

Thus we will find in the present those opportunities for the entity to work under the very same ac-

tivities in which there were those measures taken
through those periods.   5008-1

Cayce advised training in law and political science
and stated that [5008] had the ability to think on his feet
and would have the opportunity to interact with individuals in high places. It was recommended that the boy
attend school near Albany, New York. Such education
would prepare him to have an active role in the affairs of
the United States. A born diplomat, he would have the
capacity to "win over" all with whom he came in contact. An appropriate spiritual upbringing was recommended along with his education and training, all
designed to help prepare him for the important role he
could play in the country's future. Innately, his talents
were in law and public service. The reading also warned
of the potential for health problems throughout his developing years.

In previous lives, [5008] had been a speechwriter in
Rome, inspiring individuals to do their part in order to
build an empire. In the Holy Land, he had been a priest,
knowledgeable about religious law and custom. In Egypt
he had served as chief spokesman for groups of people
and had assisted in the preparation of individuals to
serve their country. Earlier, he had been one of the first
children born to the offspring of Noah after the deluge,
and had been responsible for the creation of laws and
regulations for individuals attempting to resettle the
land.

After receiving the information, the boy's mother
wrote: " . . . [5008]'s reading is lovely and will be our greatest guide." Sixteen years later, the mother added: "[5008]'s
reading has been a great help to me and still is. He has
just come into his own after a long struggle through his
entire childhood and is quite or rather truly a magnifi-
cent figure now. He has one more year at Mt. Hermon

School and hopes to go to college in a more southern part of U.S."

No additional reports are on file.

Reynolds, Sir Joshua
1723-1792
Case 4098

The author of the classic *Discourses* on the principles of art, Reynolds was the leading portrait painter of the eighteenth century. Trained under Thomas Hudson, he soon attracted his own enormous following. He served as first president of the Royal Academy and was knighted and appointed as Painter-in-Ordinary to the king. He is best known for his amazing ability to bring his subjects to life and his use of classical devices in the style of the grand masters.

For a nine-month-old boy, Edgar Cayce described innate talents as both a musician and an artist. He recommended that the child be given musical training and be encouraged to practice for the next eighteen years: "An exceptional musician, especially piano. If the opportunity is given here we may have to the musical world of America what Sir Joshua Reynolds was in his field—for it is the same entity." (4098-1)

Although the child was stubborn and inclined to have his own way, Cayce advised the parents to use music to help work with his temper:

Do give the opportunity for music. Let the entity listen to and be guided by, not that character of music that is of the passing fancy but that which builds harmony, that which builds the bridge between the sublime and the finite—or from the infinite to the finite mind. Cultivate these more often in the body-mind as it unfolds. Thus we will find less and less of this tendency for headstrongness.

4098-1

In the Holy Land, [4098] had helped individuals experience oneness of mind through song and the use of stringed instruments. In one of the temples in ancient Egypt, he had worked with the music of stringed instruments as well. Cayce stated that the child's future was entirely dependent upon his training during his formative years.

In 1960, when the boy was a senior in high school, it was reported: "[4098] is working after school hours and on Saturdays for a local TV concern. Making very good money for a child—part of which he is trying to save toward his college education. He graduates in the spring and at the present time says his strong leaning is toward mechanical drawing or architecture. He is extremely talented along these lines—can sit down and just sketch off anything with his hands."

The last note in the file is from his sister who reported in 1968 that [4098] was planning to go to Georgia Tech to study engineering, although he still wasn't sure what he wanted to do with his life.

Rochambeau, Jean Baptiste
1725-1807
Case 2246

An officer who had made a name for himself in both the War of Austrian Succession and the Seven Years' War, Rochambeau is best known for his role as the French general who helped the American forces defeat the British at Yorktown in 1781. Louis XVI dispatched him with approximately 6,000 troops to help George Washington's forces. Under Washington's command, he remained inactive for almost a year while he waited in vain for more

French troops to join the conflict. Finally, he persuaded Washington to alter plans. Their successful attack on Yorktown against the British virtually ended the war.

A seventy-year-old retired professor became interested in the work of Edgar Cayce. At first his interest seemed focused on the possibility of Texas land speculation and finding oil, but he soon obtained a life reading. During the course of his reading, he was encouraged to keep the faith he had discovered in Antioch as a Roman statistician during the time of the apostles. He was reminded of the purpose he had held to in Atlantis when he had assisted individuals in discovering their personal relationship with the Creator. [2246] was also advised to keep the perseverance he had found during the American Revolution.

> Before this, then, we find that the activities of the entity were in the land of the present nativity; yet of French birth was the entity then and came with Marquis de Lafayette (or Jean Paul Lafayette) as a defender of liberty in this land—Count Rochambeau . . .
>
> The abilities as an instructor, a teacher, are the influences from a portion of the entity's experience through that sojourn . . . the love of freedom, the love of ease, the love of beauty—yea, the love of women—arise from those experiences in that sojourn . . .   2246-1

In Rome, his name had been Philen and he had kept detailed reports of the activities of the disciples. At the same time, he had been fascinated with "those things of an agricultural and of a mineral nature." According to Cayce, some of Philen's reports were still contained in the Vatican library. [2246] was told that he had innate talents as a writer, a healer, a teacher, even an orator. The reading's advice was that he needed to focus his energies into spirituality—a spirituality he could live rather than preach.

After receiving the reading, professor [2246] wrote:

> It has had a curious effect upon me. I feel as though I had let the Count de Rochambeau down by accomplishing so little in this incarnation for the good of humanity. In one way, my life has been unconsciously selfish for I have been apparently more intent on developing my own mentality from probably a vain idea of showing forth the glory of God, as far as it may have been revealed to me, and I do *not* feel that I have lived up to what I seemed to have been.

He was deeply grateful for his friendship with Edgar and Gertrude Cayce and promised to do everything he could to further the ideals and purposes of the A.R.E. for the rest of his life.

Years later, in 1975, a letter was sent to the Vatican library requesting information about any manuscripts that had been written by a Roman statistician named Philen. A response came from the Vatican stating that because of the status of their vast cataloging project, finding such information would be almost impossible at that time.

Rolfe, John
1585-1622
Case 2661

Best known as the husband of Pocahontas, John Rolfe was one of the first English settlers in Virginia. He is credited with developing the best strain of tobacco for Virginia sometime after arriving at the Jamestown colony in 1610, for which he became extremely successful. He married the Indian princess Pocahontas in 1614 and took her to England for a visit. (See also "Pocahontas.") After her death, he returned to America and was killed by Indians a few years later.

In 1931, the grandmother of a nine-year-old boy was told that her grandson's future vocation lay with the sea and navigation. Apparently he had an innate longing to be involved with the sea and foreign lands. In his life just previous, he had sailed the ocean to settle in the New World:

> In the one then before this we find in that land of the present nativity, and during that period when there was the settling of the land in and about that now known as Virginia—or virgin land. The entity then among those peoples who settled in the land, and among those of the nobles of the land, and one who sacrificed self—in some manners and respects; for the entity was in the name Rolfe.   2661-1

Previously, he had been among the early Christians where he had learned to judge what was spiritually valuable and truthful—he possessed the same talent in the present. In Atlantis, he had been one of those who had emigrated from the main continent to South America. Those responsible for the child were encouraged to provide him with spiritual precepts as well as to be cautious of his physical condition, especially as it pertained to his throat and throat membranes, for they were extremely sensitive. (Could this perhaps be from his work with tobacco during his Jamestown incarnation?) Cayce also stated that the boy would seem to attract those individuals in his life who had money.

No follow-up reports from the boy's upbringing or adulthood are on file.

Romulus
ca. 750 B.C.
Case 5618

In Roman mythology, Romulus, along with his twin brother, Remus, are regarded as the founders of Rome. Ordered to be killed as infants, they were set afloat on the Tiber River and came to rest at the future site of Rome. There a she-wolf and a woodpecker suckled and fed them. Eventually, herdsmen adopted the two. They grew to adulthood and laid claim to the city. Eventually Romulus killed his brother, consolidated his power, and the city of Rome was named after him. According to legend, Romulus is credited with the creation of the senate, the division of the Roman people into tribal units, and the acquisition and rape of the Sabine women.

Rather than this story simply being a myth, Edgar Cayce told a doctor of osteopathy and enthusiast of the Edgar Cayce work that he had been Romulus as well as Louis XVI, king of France.

In the one before this we find in that of the entity Romulus, who assisted in the building of that now known as Rome, and the entity lost and gained in that period, for in the labors there came success, and in success came self-aggrandizement, which gave to the entity that of the oppression to others. In the present urge we find the entity not able to countenance, stand, or bear, oppression in any manner or form, whether in the animal, mineral or vegetable kingdom.   5618-8

Cayce told Dr. [5618] that rather than choosing power in this lifetime, which could have been misused, he had instead chosen to be of service to others. In fact, in most of [5618]'s incarnations he had chosen to serve people in whatever position he found himself. For that reason, Dr. [5618] had overcome much of the self-aggrandizement that had been a part of his incarnation as Romulus. (See also "Louis XVI.")

Rubens, Peter Paul
1577-1640
Case 1123

Considered the most renowned Flemish baroque painter of his day, Rubens is now credited with redirecting much of European art by combining the traditions of Flemish with Italian Renaissance painting. A master by the age of twenty-one, he spent considerable time painting pieces for the Roman Catholic Church. His phenomenal productivity as a painter was interrupted from time to time when he served as a diplomat for Spain. Although his early career often drew from classical mythology, during the final decade of his life, he became fascinated with portraits, scenes from everyday life, and landscapes.

In 1936, a physician-mother requested a life reading for her twelve-year-old son. In her correspondence she made note of the fact that [1123], her son, "seems to have a leaning towards art—he wants to draw all the time." While giving the reading, Cayce stated that the child was extremely sensitive and prone to daydream—he would never be called practical. The boy was encouraged to become a channel for expressing the glory of the Creative Forces. Innately, he also possessed talents with writing and could easily express emotions through writing or speaking.

In terms of a career, the reading suggested a field of work in "Either interior or exterior decorating, or an artist along these lines . . . " In his lifetime just previous to the present, he had been an aid to the surveyors who laid out the city of Washington, D.C. From that experience, he had an innate ability with landscaping and the beautifying of lands and roadways. The boy's interest in art had come from his life as Peter Paul Rubens:

> Then in the name Rheubens [Rubens?] the entity made for much of that from which the Flemish paintings became the expressions that were given upon the greens, or those manners of reproduction in painting of folklore, of folk expressions, of the home, of the various periods in the experiences of groups and individuals of certain classes or types.
>
> 1123-1

In a lifetime in Persia, [1123] had tried to help salvage things of a spiritual and emotional value from a city that was on the verge of destruction. In Egypt, he had been an Atlantean who had excelled at decorating the various temples. In the present, the boy would be more drawn to "the beauty of a blossom, the buzzing of a bee," rather than to such things as mathematics or logic. His weakness was becoming too easily discouraged at times or too enthusiastic at others. For that reason, his parents were encouraged to give their child a balanced and orderly life, physically, mentally, and spiritually—especially during the next three to four years of his development.

Over the next few years, his mother obtained physical readings for childhood problems. Also, in 1941, during a mental-spiritual reading for herself, the boy's mother asked several questions in regard to how she could best help her son. She was told that much of her work as a mother should be commended thus far and that she simply needed to continue to raise him with Christlike principles.

In 1943, the boy's mother wrote: "Our son [1123] is in the engineering branch of the service now." The last correspondence on file is from 1950 when the mother, Dr. [1125], wrote to say that she was making plans to visit her son, [1123], his wife, and her new granddaughter.

Smith, John
ca. 1580-1631
Case 415

As explorer and leader, John Smith helped establish the first permanent English colony at Jamestown in 1607. His roles also included those of cartographer and writer, and his vivid descriptions of the beauty and abundance of the New World encouraged additional English settlers to come to America. Known for helping the new settlers focus on their own survival, he directed the building of homes, began trade with the Indians, and continued to draw maps of the surrounding areas. In 1607, he was ambushed by Indians and was reportedly saved from execution by the chief's thirteen-year-old daughter, Pocahontas. (See also "Pocahontas.") At one point he tried to establish another colony in New England but was unsuccessful. He returned to England and wrote and talked about the New World for the rest of his life.

A four-year-old boy was told in 1933 that he would be easily influenced by love. His career and training were suggested as "either toward law, religious thought or ministering, in lecturing, or the like." Possessing high mental abilities, [415], according to his reading, was also prone to be hardheaded and stubborn. However, these tendencies could be overcome through kindness, reason, gentleness, and love.

As far as past lives were concerned, in the one just previous to the present, he had been Captain John Smith:

Before this the entity was in that period, in and

about the present land of nativity, when there were the first settlings in the land . . . John Smith.

In the activities the entity through the experience gained and lost, though often counted among those that acted in a very peculiar capacity. Yet the entity was among those that aided, yet in favor with those in power; and the entity had the abilities of being able to direct through those experiences so as to bring for the entity itself an advancement in soul's activity. For, in the greater portion of the experience, even though it may be termed by many as to have been rather the activity to bring the plaudit of the greater numbers, the entity's activities were such as to give self for those things that others might be aided and gain in their experience through the sojourn.

As to the present activity from that period, there will be a tendency for the entity to explore into [uncharted] fields. Not necessarily so much in the material things as into the mental experiences and the activities of same.   415-1

Before his incarnation as Smith, [415] had acted in the capacity of a lawyer during the rule of Alfred the Great. From that experience came a quick intellect, as well as "the ability to argue anything that may be presented to the body . . ." In Persia, he had helped to organize new settlers to the country into law-abiding citizens. Eventually, he also became one of the first judges, helping to establish lawfulness among the various peoples that had been brought together in one land. During a lifetime in ancient Egypt, [415] had helped to bring order among people who were rebelling against the king. From that experience came talents as a speaker, a lawyer, and a minister. Cayce stated that regardless of whether [415] became a minister or a lawyer, he would, in all likelihood, act in both capacities in whatever career he chose.

As years passed and the boy grew up, he received a series of physical readings for various ailments, including scarlet fever, for which the boy and his family were convinced that Mr. Cayce had saved his life. In 1940, at the age of eleven, [415] wrote that he was very interested in drawing maps and discovering new things. He added: "I want to carry out my life reading and be the best lawyer or whatever I should be."

At the age of eighteen, he wrote an article for the *A.R.E. Bulletin* describing the accuracy of his life reading. It said, in part:

You may be interested in knowing how accurately the reading described me. Remember that I was only four years old. Here is the list of character traits mentioned in various places in the reading: "temper, hardheadedness, tendency to argue about everything, leadership, easily influenced by love (spiritual or purely carnal)." This fits me all right, especially "the tendency to argue" and "hardheadedness." And I guess you could say that my election to several offices in school and young people's activities shows some leadership. Mr. Cayce didn't see me at the time of the reading, but even if he had I was just four.

Probably one of the most unusual parts of my life reading was a prediction that came true. [Cayce had predicted that between the twelfth through the fifteeth year, (415) would be ruled by mental anger/ frustration, causing much concern for his parents.] It was that time in my life when I began to have trouble with teachers in school and it ended up with my leaving school for a time in my fifteeth year. Naturally this caused my family considerable worry. Anger played a big part in all this trouble . . .

There are parts of the reading that fit me better

than anyone else knows. I have just begun to realize how strong some of the urges can be. Being warned about them helps a great deal. It has enabled my family to understand and help me, and in the future it will help me meet myself . . . It is a responsibility, a challenge, a great deal to live up to— because I am just an average boy who knows more than the boy next door about himself and what he should accomplish.

Throughout his teen years, [415] had become very interested in electronics and had taken various courses in that field. He was married in 1959 and his stepfather reported in 1965 that "[415] is now field engineer working in a supervisory capacity, in a big electronics firm." He and his wife had three children, two girls and a boy. Physically, [415] had developed a problem with enteritis and had to be extremely careful with the foods he was eating because of the effect they had on his digestion and eliminations.

The final report on file is from his stepfather who updated A.R.E. on his son's physical condition in 1967, diagnosed as ulcerative colitis. At the time, [415] was still employed as a field engineer in electronics.

Tacitus, Cornelius
ca. 55-ca. 117
Case 2294

Considered one of the great Roman historians, Tacitus was also a Roman senator. In addition to being a popular orator, he was considered a masterful writer of prose. After serving in various roles as a public official, he devoted his life to writing the history of Rome from the death of Augustus (A.D. 14) to the death of Domitian (A.D. 96).

A one-month-old boy received a life reading at the request of his father. Apparently this soul had experienced two notable lifetimes in history: one as the brilliant orator and politician, Patrick Henry, and the other as the Roman senator and historian, Tacitus. (See also "Henry, Patrick.")

Before that the entity was in the Roman land, when there were the needs for those who were capable and able to give expressions to the desires of the peoples, as well as of those in authority—that is, as to that chosen to be expressed by the common people.

Thus in the present we will find the entity inclined to seek out those of various positions or conditions in life. These tendencies also should be guided—not curbed so much, but the whys and wherefores of these given or reasoned with the entity concerning, in the early developing period; else we may find those tendencies to associate with those who are questionable characters—for the entity may easily be turned into those directions of using its abilities that would not be the constructive force.

Hence the needs for the spiritual welfare of the entity to be considered during its early periods of development.

For, the entity then was not only the historian but the speaker, as well as the poet. All of these will find their expressions in the present activities of the entity, for the entity then was in the name Tacitus.

2294-1

Velazquez, Diego de Silva
1599-1660
Case 4361

A major Spanish painter of the seventeeth century, Velazquez is known for his great contribution to Western art in the areas of perspective, space, light, and color. Apprenticed at the age of twelve, he became an independent master by the time he was eighteen. At the age of twenty-four, he became court painter to King Philip IV, where he served for the rest of his life. He is known for his brilliant portraits, religious works, and equestrian portraits.

In 1924, in one of the earliest life readings, a thirty-three-year-old man was told that innately he was idealistic and emotional. Additional tendencies included being a wanderer, temperamental and nervous, and always appearing to be just short of attaining that which he had set out to do.

> In the influences of the forces exercised in the physical, we find the body in physical well, and is that that brings rather the influence of expectancy in development physical, mental and moral, and always the financial in the more beautiful side. Hence the turn towards that of artistic forces, and the entity's development upon the earth plane has been in that of art forces, for in the plane just before this we find this was in that force known as Valesque [Velazquez?] at that period and time.   4361-1

In Persia, [4361] had been a nomad, which accounted for his wandering tendency in the present. In Atlantis he had been both artist and decorator. The reading stated that innately he was drawn to the study of art as well as metaphysics, and the vocation recommended for him was in the field of art.

No follow-up reports are on file.

Veronica, Saint
ca. A.D. 30
Case 489

According to legend, Veronica was a pious woman who was moved with pity at the sight of Jesus carrying His cross to Golgotha. She gave Him her kerchief so that He might wipe the sweat from His brow. When Jesus handed the cloth back to her, it had become miraculously imprinted with the image of His face.

A fifty-three-year-old woman was told in 1934 that throughout her sojourns in the earth, she had developed the qualities of gentleness, kindness, and sympathy. She possessed the abilities of a peacemaker and had often been able to end an argument and bring people together. In her life just previous, she had been in England and held to her religious convictions and beliefs in spite of persecution. In Egypt, she had helped disseminate truths, especially those related to healing. In Judea, she had been a student of the Essenes and, according to Cayce, the mother of Stephen, who would become the first martyr. Her name at the time had been Veronicani:

> With the coming of the trial and the crucifixion of the Master, when there were the periods of turmoil among those that had been the followers and teachers, and when the Roman pontiff under Cleodius disbanded or broke up the place of refuge during those periods when the trial was being brought about or being planned by the peoples, the entity then suffered the persecutions; not only because of the associations but for the heritage of the land or peoples from which the entity had been a native

and a sojourner and had gained much for the native friends and associates.

When the trial arose, and when there was the preparation for the burial of the body, the entity Veronicani bathed the face of the Master. And thence arose much of that which has come as an ability in the healing and in the ministry of the soul force to those with or for whom the entity may pray or seek to aid in an hour of turmoil.   489-3

Cayce told her that throughout her lifetime in Palestine, she had been a dedicated supporter of the small Christian sect. In the present, she was encouraged to minister to the needs, the wants, and the weaknesses of others, just as she had done in the past. She was also advised to continue sharing her truth with those around her, for it was an innate desire of her soul. A very caring individual, she was later called by Edgar Cayce, "one of the loveliest persons I think I have ever had the pleasure to know."

Deeply appreciative of the ways in which the readings had helped her and her family, [489] contributed to the Cayce work over the years and referred many individuals for their own readings. Family tragedy struck several times—her husband died in 1939 and her son was killed in an automobile accident in 1940. She remarried and remained a supporter of A.R.E.

In 1957, a routine mailing was sent to her and returned marked "deceased."

Vinci, Leonardo
1690-1730
Case 2897
(not Leonardo da Vinci)

Vinci was an Italian composer, whose first known

work was a comic opera. In addition to his forty operas, he also composed oratorios, motets, and a great deal of music for church masses. His work is known for its dramatic vigor and its directness of expression. Reportedly, he killed himself by poisoning.

In 1929, Cayce told a thirty-three-year-old musical conductor and band leader that he had once been a composer. A pianist and a Catholic, [2897] was interested in reincarnation, nature, and philosophy. Passionate in his work, he was told that innately he had the ability to sway people's emotions. In his lifetime in Italy, his name had been Antonio Leonardo Vinci:

> . . . in that period when there was both music, song, painting, and the like, in the entity's endeavors, and the entity brought to self in that experience much of that in the period that brought consternation, through the gratification of selfish desires, and to the aggrandizement of selfish interests, *belittling* the body through that experience to the satisfying of the elements that act through the imaginative forces of selfish interests; bringing into the experience of the entity those of dissatisfying influences, ending in the manner—as was seen—in self's own destruction. Bringing then, as it does in the present, those of the influences that bring dissatisfaction at times with individuals, and with those influences that would bind in any manner, as relating to *bound* relationships with individuals; yet *gaining* in the experience *in* the ability to apply self in a *physical* manner as to any of the arts. As the entity then called the great artist, so today he may be called— in this experience—the artist in more than one direction.   2897-1

In Greece, he had served as a counselor and had acquired his great love of nature. In Egypt, he had also served as a counselor to the ruler and had also created music for use in the temples. In Atlantis, he had been a ruler and had gained his love for philosophy and the mysteries of the unknown. The reading stated that his talents were varied and, in the present, he "may become either the writer, the musician, the painter, or the one accomplished in either of these."

One of the first reports on file is from 1931, when his band was touring the country. As time passed, he became a band leader of some renown. In addition to his work with music, he later wrote various books on the subjects of astrology, numerology, and prophecy. In his book on astrology, he even included his life reading, and Gladys Davis noted in 1975 that he didn't mind people knowing about his present identity as Vincent Lopez. The final report on file is his obituary, a portion of which is included here:

> MIAMI (AP)—Band leader Vincent Lopez, who began remote radio broadcasts of orchestras in the 1920s and whose bands included some of the nation's top musicians for 58 years, is dead at 80 . . . Lopez was noted for his abilities on the piano, which he learned to play from his father, a onetime naval bandmaster. Lopez originally was headed for a clerical vocation, but dropped out of a monastery at age 15 and got a job playing piano in a Brooklyn saloon.
>
> . . . he established a radio first with a live performance in the studio of WJZ and later made the first radio remote music pickup. His theme song was "Nola," and his trademark opening for every radio broadcast was "Hello, everybody, Lopez speaking."
>
> . . . Among the top musicians who at one time

played for him were Tommy Dorsey and Xavier Cougat. Lopez also was instrumental in aiding the careers of Glenn Miller, Artie Shaw and singer Abby Lane.

A sideline was astrology and numerology . . .

Washington, Martha
1731-1802
Case 2459

Best known as the wife of George Washington, Martha Washington became a widow after her husband, Daniel Parke Custis, a wealthy Virginia planter, died. The mother of four surviving children prior to her second marriage, she did not have additional children with Washington. Although she took no part in politics, Martha was known by her contemporaries as a gracious hostess and a sensible woman.

The mother of a three-year-old girl was told that her daughter was strong in body, mind, and purpose. Innately, however, [2459] would be inconsistent in her activities with money. Possessing an artistic temperament, the child would also love history and be a leader in whatever direction her life took her. Inclined to have her own way, Cayce stated that she would be able to "wrap most of the opposite sex about its own finger . . . " The reading recommended a vocation as a decorator or a designer—a talent she had acquired (along with her temperament) in Greece. Most notably, Cayce stated that [2459] would probably once again become the companion of a leader in this country, for she had once been Martha Washington:

For, the entity eventually became the wife of him known as the father of his country.

In that experience the entity was in that position

to know the needs of the many varied kinds, characters, positions and places of activity; yet, as may be gathered much from the life of the entity through that period, ever an example as well as an inspiration for *all* of those peoples of the day . . .

The entity was among the first to become burdened with financial responsibility, as would be called in the present; yet little or none of its own making, but by choice of association, by choice of companionship and activity.

Too little stress has been given as to how this entity, Martha, led in creating that inspiration for not only her companions through that period but with her fortitude and strength brought inspiration to those who were in the position of might and power by their very electorate vote to set the policies of this new land.   2459-1

During a lifetime in Palestine, she had also been among the companions of those in authority and had known the holy women, the disciples, and Jesus. In Egypt, she had been one of the daughters of the High Priest and active in one of the temples. Cayce told the parents to provide the child with a spiritual upbringing and reacquaint her with the material she had once known in Palestine. They were encouraged to seek further guidance for the girl when she was twelve or thirteen.

No reports about who or what the child became as an adult are on file.

Wesley, Charles
1707-1788
Case 2458

Although an important minister, Wesley is regarded

primarily as England's greatest hymn writer. Educated at Oxford, he and his brother, John, were responsible for founding and spreading the Methodist movement after both had encountered personal spiritual experiences. Although Wesley spent a short time in the United States, his and his brother's High Church views were seen as extreme by the Colonists. He returned to England and continued his ministry until 1756 when he devoted his time to hymn writing. He is responsible for more than 5,000 hymns, including "Hark, the Herald Angels Sing."

An eleven-year-old Protestant boy was told that he had great abilities that could be turned into positive or negative directions. Innately, he could be too dictatorial, but at the same time he had a great connection to spiritual forces. The boy's reading was brief in nature and provided only one previous incarnation that was greatly influencing his present. According to Cayce, [2458] had been Charles Wesley. In addition to his abilities as a minister and a hymn writer, the reading stated that Wesley had also been extremely psychic.

In terms of the child's upbringing, Cayce advised the parents to study the life of Wesley and to analyze that individual's purposes and abilities. Principally, they were also told to "Keep the entity from that of self-confusion, self-domination; and build the desire to serve others— for that is the duty of each soul." (2458-1)

No follow-up reports are on file.

Whitney, Eli
1765-1825
Case 2012

An inventor and manufacturer, Eli Whitney is best known for the cotton gin, but his advancements with the development of interchangeable parts in a manufacturing process revolutionized ideas for mass production. A graduate of Yale, he served as a teacher until his invention of the cotton gin, which separated the cotton seed from the fiber. As a result, cotton became the principal cash crop of the southern states. Because of copyright infringements, he was not financially successful until he applied his mass-manufacturing ideas to the production of muskets.

A twenty-six-year-old physicist requested a life reading in 1939. Possessing unusual abilities and intellect, he was told that innately he could bring into the human experience that which would add "weal or . . . woe" to the lives of others.

> As to the appearances or sojourns of the entity in the material plane:
>
> Before this we find the entity was that one who symbolized to the land of the entity's present sojourn the ability to separate the good from the bad in cotton, as well as that which stabilized parts for moving mechanical instruments, as well as guns and ammunitions and parts for same.
>
> These were the work of the entity through that experience or sojourn—as one Whitney.
>
> In the experience the entity gained and lost— gained throughout in the desire to make for creative influences and forces in the experiences of others, without the thought of the great material gains for self. Those as were of constructive creation brought creative forces. Those as brought destructive influences brought negative forces in the experience of the entity.   2012-1

In Rome, he had acted as a type of analyst and counselor, establishing the potential productivity of various lands and places. In Atlantis, he had been a record-keeper and had preserved much information before the final destruction of the land. From that experience came an awareness that anything that was needed in the present had been a part of the past. He was encouraged to direct his energies into the spirit of good, rather than doing things simply so that good would be spoken of him.

He was told that his vocation could be found in anything that used his creative genius for the preservation of life in all its phases.

After receiving the reading, [2012] wrote to say that he found most of the information quite plausible, "However, I feel that psychic phenomena must be established on a more objective basis before I can honestly accept its teachings."

In 1939, while serving in the Pacific, [2012], according to his mother's letter, had an invention in mind that he hoped to follow through with after his tour of duty; however, no additional reference to the invention is contained within the files. In 1940, he was placed in command of some of the laboratories of a large manufacturing company. In 1956, his mother mentioned that all four of her sons had served in World War II and all returned unharmed.

In 1973, a routine mailing was sent to [2012]'s last known address and was returned "undeliverable."

Willard, Frances Elizabeth Caroline
1839-1898
Case 2015

Frances Willard was a driving force in both the women's and temperance movements of the nineteenth century. She was a brilliant orator, a successful lobbyist, and extremely devoted to human rights, helping the poor and underprivileged. She founded the World's Woman's Christian Temperance Union in 1883 and became a leader of the national Prohibition Party. A teacher by training, she became president of the Evanston College for Ladies in Illinois. In addition to temperance, she was an advocate for woman's suffrage and safety in industry.

In October of 1939, a couple obtained a life reading for their baby girl when the child was only fifteen days old. Previously, they had procured physical readings for her dealing with baby care. They would obtain additional physical readings for this child during her upbringing. The girl's life reading stated that she had been Frances Willard:

> Before this we find the entity was Frances Willard, who was active in creating those influences for temperance, as well as for the underprivileged.
>
> Hence we will find that these will be a part of the present experience. Even in its early years there will be the desire to take sides with all of the little colored children, as well as all the little poor children about the entity; not caring for others.   2015-3

In France, she had been the child of royalty. In Jerusalem, she had helped those who were outcasts, wanting to give away all that she possessed. In Persia she had been a nurse, and from that lifetime she had acquired both physical beauty and a keenness of mind. In ancient Egypt, she had been involved with purification in one of the temples. According to the reading, if the child were guided aright, her abilities would manifest into constructive channels that would help others.

According to the reports, she was not told of her connection to Frances Willard until she was sixteen. At the age of thirty-one, [2015] began to compile the striking similarities between her own life and the life of the nineteenth-century woman. The data became so convincing that author Jeffrey Furst worked with her to write a book detailing their investigation and its results. The book was called *The Return of Frances Willard* (1971).

In addition to physical appearance, beliefs, desires, and manner of speech, [2015]'s life paralleled the life of Frances Willard in many ways. Just a few of those similarities include the fact that at the age of three or four, [2015] had demanded to be taken to the polls with her father to vote. She was constantly singing Frances Willard's favorite hymn "Rock of Ages." While she was growing up, she frequently lectured to invisible audiences. She had also been attracted to the same artwork that had once hung in Frances Willard's home.

One of the last reports on file states that [2015] had continued to help people with her life. At the time of the report, she was a volunteer social worker at a day-care center for underprivileged children.

Xenophon
ca. 430-ca. 354 B.C.
Case 2903

A commander and Greek historian, Xenophon was a student of Socrates in his youth and later joined the military. Disliking the democratic institutions in Athens into which he had been born, he eventually joined with the Spartans against the Greeks—an act for which he was eventually banished from the city. After his service in the Spartan army, he devoted himself to writing and hunting. His best-known writings include the *Hellenica,* which is a history of Greece from 411 to 362 B.C. His biographical work includes information on Socrates as well as a romantic biography of Cyrus the Great.

In 1925, a life insurance representative was told that he had once been Xenophon:

In the one before this, we find in the days of the

wars in the Grecian forces. The entity then in that of him who led the forces in the raids in the Western portion of the country. Also leading the peoples to the higher understanding of self, and seeking to educate them in that which would give the better influence in their homes. Then in the name Xenophon, and in this we find in the present the urge and ability to so direct the lives of others that the best may come to them. The detrimental forces coming from these being that of the warriors in the flesh, being fearful of same.   2903-1

Mr. [2903] was also told that he had been Oliver Cromwell. (See also "Cromwell, Oliver.")

AFTERWORD

Although approximately seventy individuals were told that they had been famous at some point in the history of the world, the Edgar Cayce readings never placed the worth of one individual over the worth of another. From the readings' perspective, every individual was very much an integral portion of the whole. In 1942, when a thirty-two-year-old woman asked whether or not a friend of hers had ever been famous in a past life, Cayce replied:

> What entity is *not* famous! What entity is *not* well known in the end! As to being worldly famous—no more than in the present; as a teacher, a helper to those along life's seeking way.   2072-10

Regardless of one's fame or lack of it in any one life, it was simply a portion of a soul existence that had been continuous since Creation. To be sure, each lifetime is an important sojourn in materiality but reincarnation is the great leveler of humankind. As far as Cayce was concerned, one's spiritual value was not determined by who she or he had been in the past, but by how that individual applied the best that she or he knew to do in the present.

Reincarnation does not suggest that individuals experience different identities throughout history which are only loosely connected one to another. Instead, life is a continuous experience of sojourns in and out of materiality, all leading to soul growth and personal transformation.

Each individual is the sum total of all that he or she has ever been. Although that totality of being has an ongoing effect upon the present, individuals are very much active cocreators in their lives' direction. The goal is soul growth, leading to an awareness of oneness with the rest of Creation. And it is achieved as each soul continually weighs the patterns and experiences of the past against the opportunities and free will of the present.

According to the readings, the success of the soul is inevitable—it is simply a matter of time.

You Can Receive Books Like This One and Much, Much More

You can begin to receive books in the *A.R.E. Membership Series* and many more benefits by joining the nonprofit Association for Research and Enlightenment, Inc., as a Sponsoring or Life member.

The A.R.E. has a worldwide membership that receives a wide variety of study aids, all aimed at assisting individuals in their spiritual, mental, and physical growth.

Every member of A.R.E. receives a copy of *Venture Inward*, the organization's bimonthly magazine; a periodic in-depth journal, *The New Millennium;* opportunity to borrow, through the mail, from a collection of more than 500 files on medical and metaphysical subjects; access to one of the world's most complete libraries on metaphysical and spiritual subjects; and opportunities to participate in conferences, international tours, a retreat-camp for children and adults, and numerous nationwide volunteer activities.

In addition to the foregoing benefits, Sponsoring and Life members also receive as gifts three books each year in the *A.R.E. Membership Series.*

If you are interested in finding out more about membership in A.R.E. and the many benefits that can assist you on your path to fulfillment, you can easily contact the Membership Department by writing Membership, A.R.E., P.O. Box 595, Virginia Beach, VA 23451-0595 or by calling **1-800-333-4499** or faxing **1-757-422-6921**.

Explore our electronic visitor's center on the Internet: http://www.are-cayce.com